EMIGRATING

The Essential Guide

Taliah
Drayak

Emigrating: The Essential Guide is also available in accessible formats for people with any degree of visual impairment. The large print edition and e-book (with accessibility features enabled) are available from Need2Know. Please let us know if there are any special features you require and we will do our best to accommodate your needs.

First published in Great Britain in 2013 by
Need2Know
Remus House
Coltsfoot Drive
Peterborough
PE2 9BF
Telephone 01733 898103
Fax 01733 313524
www.need2knowbooks.co.uk

Contents

Introduction 5

Chapter 1 Relocating 9

Chapter 2 Residency 19

Chapter 3 Employment 27

Chapter 4 Property 35

Chapter 5 Finances 43

Chapter 6 Education 51

Chapter 7 Culture 59

Chapter 8 Lifestyle 67

Chapter 9 Healthcare 77

Chapter 10 Transport 85

Glossary 91

Appendix 95

Help List 99

Book List 103

References 105

Introduction

Britain is going through the most dramatic levels of emigration in recent history. The number of British people emigrating with the intention of long-term relocation rose to over 350,000 in 2011. This is the equivalent to one person leaving every 90 seconds.

There are many reasons motivating British nationals to emigrate. Over 50% of British Expats have relocated to one of four countries: Australia, New Zealand, France and Spain. While warmer climates may play a role in the decision to move, many people are choosing to take advantage of work opportunities. Governments around the world have skill shortages to fill, and this may provide an excellent opportunity for someone struggling to build their career in recession-hit Britain.

Cultural changes have played a significant role in British emigrants choosing to leave their homeland. Migration statistic reports have recorded over 590,000 immigrants came into the UK. This influx of people has seen changes in employment as well as having heightened demographic and cultural transformations in local communities. The overall effect is that the population of the UK is increasing by a city the size of Bristol every year. The dramatic growth in population is resulting in a lot of pressure being placed on housing and public services.

For some, the potential to achieve a higher standard of living in a country with a lower population density is incredibly appealing. Emigrating can provide the opportunity to leave a long commute behind, step out of the rat race and build a comfortable life in a place where the cost of living is significantly lower. In some parts of Canada, for example, a large four-bedroomed property with 10 acres can be purchased for under £10,000. It is unlikely that a single-room apartment in London could be purchased for less than twice this price.

Lifestyle is another important factor which influences the choice to emigrate. Being able to move abroad to a place where you can climb mountains, own your own smallholding or have access to private sandy beaches is very attractive. For many, it can be intimidating to leave your familiar and cherished

'Governments around the world have skill shortages to fill, and this may provide an excellent opportunity for someone struggling to build their career in recession-hit Britain.'

birth place. However, it is worth noting that you would not be alone. In 41 different countries around the world, there are over 10,000 British nationals who have emigrated on a long-term basis.

Emigration is about combining an exciting adventure with the opportunity to achieve a higher quality of life. Modern technology has made emigration easier than ever by allowing families and friends to affordably maintain contact with each other. Travel is flexible and affordable, which encourages regular return visits for anyone who develops a touch of homesickness.

If you have ever considered applying for emigration in order to chase your dreams, this informative, easy-to-read book is written for you. Packed with the most up-to-date information on everything from choosing a destination, planning your move to organising your finances, this book will guide you through how to arrange your emigration.

There is no need to be daunted by government forms, visa applications or banking abroad. This book will take you step by step through the process of applying for emigration all the way through to naturalisation. Chapter 2 will help you to identify common difficulties and hurdles to ensure your application process goes smoothly.

One chapter is devoted to looking for a property, including help and advice on buying a home abroad, as well as guidance on how to make money from investment properties. Another chapter will focus on employment opportunities, applying for jobs and starting your own business. There is advice and information on culture, lifestyles and healthcare. The aim of this book is to provide you with a well-rounded and complete overview of all the information you will need to successful navigate emigration easily and enjoyably.

Acknowledgements

I would like to thank the all the people from six international British consulates, who took the time to answer my questions and allowed me to verify information, when a document was not publicly available. I would also like to say thank you to friends and family abroad for the sharing your experiences, which has made this book a richer and more meaningful guide.

Disclaimer

This book is for general advice on emigration and isn't intended to replace professional advice. Emigration can only be achieved by following the laws of immigration that are laid out by the government in your destination country. This book is not able to cover every minor detail of those rules and regulations, and it is important that you research and follow the guidelines as carefully as possible. Should you have any concerns while on your emigration journey, contact the UK-based consulate of your destination country. If you develop any concerns once you have departed, then you should contact your British consulate, who will be able to answer any questions you might have. All information was correct at the time of going to press. Local information is subject to change, so it is important to contact the citizenship and immigration department of the local government before submitting your application.

Chapter One

Relocating

Choosing a destination

The decision to emigrate is never any easy one to make. Leaving behind your home, family, friends and all your known comforts to leap into the unfamiliar is daunting for even the bravest and most adventurous of people. There are many good reasons to leave, and each emigrant will have their own unique reasons for their decision.

The choice of destinations does not make the decision any easier. There are several prominent countries that are worth considering. Most people will emigrate to a place which they either have or feel an established connection to. Nonetheless, it is worth having a look at all your options before making a choice. Investigate your potential country thoroughly and ponder at least one other option. The perfect opportunity often presents itself when we least expect it.

The sheer scope of possible destinations is far too broad to be fully considered here. As such this book will aim to examine the seven most common emigration destinations in detail. Nonetheless, the information in each chapter will be comprehensive and relative to most destinations.

'The decision to emigrate is never any easy one to make.'

Australia

According to various surveys, Australia is the most popular place for British emigrants. Its strong economy, and its constant need for skilled labour and tradesmen have resulted in a comfortable transition for those who have chosen to make the move. British Expats recommend the schools and public services, such as hospitals, as being outstanding. The excellent climate and laid-back culture offer a relaxing place to live.

Canada

Canada is a welcoming nation for immigrants. There is a large labour shortage in many industries, which has resulted in immigrants with key skills being encouraged through relaxed laws and financial incentives. Low population levels and wide open spaces has resulted in low property prices, and close-knit communities. Canada is made up of over 20% first generation immigrants and has a reputation for offering newcomers a warm welcome. Canada is a peaceful country that is intensely protective of its environment. Family and outdoor activities are both central to Canadian culture.

'There is a large labour shortage in many industries, which has resulted in immigrants with key skills being encouraged through relaxed laws and financial incentives.'

Spain

Spain's relaxed immigration laws have seen a large influx of immigrants from the UK in recent years. There is an abundance of employment in the agricultural, construction and service industries. Frequent and inexpensive flights back to Britain create easy opportunities for visiting family, and the excellent climate is fantastic for outdoor activities. English is not widely spoken. However, it may be the perfect opportunity to stop putting off learning a second language, and become immersed in a new and exciting culture.

New Zealand

New Zealand is a popular place to visit and relocate. The beautiful country boasts mild weather and affordable housing. The low tax rates are appealing; meanwhile the generous annual leave allowances combined with reasonable working hours has harmonised a healthy work life balance with a low cost of living. English is widely spoken. With low crime rates and a family-friendly culture, it is easy to see why New Zealand is appealing.

France

Close to home, France is a popular choice for those wishing to emigrate. The beautiful countryside and rich culture are exceptionally appealing. The south coast offers warmer weather, while the country's infrastructure is very similar to the UK. With a basic understanding of French being taught routinely in UK schools, it is an easy language in which to accomplish fluency.

Dubai

Prosperous and warm is a good description of Dubai. The hot, arid climate is excellent for anyone who dreams of escaping the cold, wet British weather. Housing is affordable and, due to steady growth, exceedingly well-paid employment is abundant. Dubai's healthcare system provides good and reliable care. There are significant cultural and legal differences which need to be researched carefully before departure.

United States

Known as the 'land of dreams', the United States of America is a vast country full of opportunity. Excellent education, employment opportunities and its iconic pop culture draw thousands of British emigrants every year. There is something for everyone in the United States, from wide open plains, rocky mountains, great lakes or Californian beaches. Whether you dream of cattle ranching in Texas, or working on Wall Street, the low population density and strong economy allow anyone who is willing to work hard to build a good life for themselves.

Planning an international move

Arranging any move is stressful but an international move is even more stressful than most. There are many arrangements to be made on both ends, and lining up dates in two different parts of the world can be tricky. Avoid moving over a bank holiday weekend and ensure you are aware of any potential holidays which may be taking place at your destination. The last thing you need on arrival to your new home is to find all the shops and car rental facilities are closed for the next three working days.

The best way to ensure everything goes smoothly is to have a plan. The following list is an overview of the items which you may need to take care of before departure. Please take a look at the complete moving checklist in the appendix. This list will provide a comprehensive overview of everything you will need to do in the six-month countdown before departure.

One to three months before departure

- Confirm removal dates with removal company.
- Sell any unwanted belongs or give them to charity.
- Book your travel arrangements.
- Check your passports are valid and arrange for renewal if necessary.
- Arrange any vaccinations required for travel.
- Contact your GP, dentist and optician, and request a copy of your medical history and prescription details.
- Collect and create copies of all your personal information. This will include: birth certificates, marriage certificates, insurance policies, legal documents, and educational certificates.
- Set up a new bank account.
- Notify your current bank and any credit providers.
- Contact the relevant authorities to advise them of your departure. These include: NHS, HM Revenue and Customs, DVLA, etc.
- Notify any insurance or policy institutions.
- Contact your service providers: telephone, water, council tax, TV licence, gas and electric, and newspapers and magazines.
- Send change of address details to all family and friends.
- Schedule any pet inoculations and kenneling.

- Apply for Royal Mail redirection.
- Contact new service providers at your new destination.
- Register with the doctor, utilities and school at your new destination.

One week before departure

- Cancel any weekly deliveries.
- Organise all travel documents and paperwork.
- Collect and label all keys.
- Organise linens and clothing for travel.
- Begin the final deep clean of your current home.
- Clear the contents of the fridge and freezer.
- Identify any items that are not going with you and dispose of them.

The day before departure

- Pack your luggage.
- Final house clean.
- Defrost freezer and fridge.
- Check utility meters, record the readings and submit them to the relevant providers.
- Pack your hand luggage.
- Charge your mobile phone.

On the day of departure

- Have a good breakfast.
- Walk through the house to ensure nothing has been forgotten.
- Switch off power and water.

▪ Hand over keys to estate agent.

Using an agency

There are many companies which offer emigration services. These are usually agencies which work with a collection of companies. They offer inclusive packages where they will professionally take over the whole process, from your emigration through immigration and will sort out every detail of your move from pets to providing a list of play parks for your children that are in close proximity to your new home.

For some, using an agency will provide relief as there is someone who will guide you through the process of changing countries. It is the agency's responsibility to ensure that all aspects are remembered and completed. A good agency may provide an excellent service. Research any agency before setting up an account. Use Internet forums and websites which provide reference checks and note problems which others may have experienced with certain agencies. However, there are a few agencies which have excellent reviews. A good personal reference is the best way to ensure the agency you choose is reliable.

'While the process may appear daunting at the outset, it is a process you are capable of accomplishing.'

The downside to agencies is the cost involved. Agencies are not cheap. It is worth remembering that while the process may appear daunting at the outset, it is a process you are capable of accomplishing. The aim of this book is to ensure you can successfully navigate this journey. Completing all the necessary documents for emigration will be discussed fully in chapter 2. It is worth being cautious in regards to any agency that suggests that you will be readily accepted into a new country by using their agency. Government offices, consulates and immigration services are there to help people. Their job is to provide guidance and assistance for free to anyone who is navigating emigration. So long as you are polite, you will find that there is an abundance of officials who are happy to answer any questions you have and will assist you without charge.

Setting up home

Once you have arrived at your destination you will undoubtedly be eager to begin setting up your new home. Approach this period with patience and consider what you need to do immediately. Many of our approaches are due to habit, and having moved to a new country it can be enjoyable to try out new ways of doing things. The initial move-in period will be taken up by arranging your home and contacting all your service providers. Try to get outside each day, to not only familiarise yourself with your new area, but to enjoy the benefits of all your hard work.

Renting

In the middle of a house move, it can be tempting to buy a property, if only to avoid ever having to face the headache of another potential house move. This is understandable, but it is worth renting a property initially in order to be able to try out an area first. The odds are good that the first area you will develop a fondness for is the first area in which you live. However, there may be many good reasons for changing areas or properties at a later date.

Equally, it is beneficial to be able to visit potential properties and locations ahead of purchase. Do not buy a property that you have not seen in person. Even simply letting a property which you have not viewed in person can be a significant risk. If possible, arrange to see your new home ahead of time, or have a trusted friend view the property on your behalf.

Removals

Removal companies can be frightfully expensive. Take a close look at how much of your stuff is actually financially worth taking with you. Everyone becomes sentimentally attached to certain items. Nonetheless, consider an item's replacement cost before putting it in a moving box. Before you hire a removal company check references and seek evidence of their insurance. A removal company is not necessarily a genuine company simply because it is listed in the Yellow Pages or because they have a website. Do your research and if at all possible, try to use a company based on personal reference.

'Government offices, consulates and immigration services are there to provide guidance and assistance for free to anyone who is navigating emigration.'

When shipping small quantities of personal items, it can be less expensive to use a shipping company. Any items which are not necessary immediately can be sent by sea, which is inexpensive if you are able to wait up to two months for your possessions to arrive.

Summing Up

- Britain is a remarkable country. Nonetheless, there are many reasons that people choose to emigrate. Always do your research and thoroughly investigate what potential opportunities are available for you.

- Plan your move well in advance. Use the comprehensive checklist, found in the appendix, to ensure you do not forget anything.

- Agencies can provide a useful service for those who lead busy lives and do not want the hassle of completing all the emigration and immigration paperwork. However, it isn't as difficult as it may first appear, and you can save a substantial fee by doing it yourself.

- Always thoroughly investigate any agency or removal company ahead of hire.

- Take your time when you first arrive at your destination. It will take a while to settle in and find your new routine.

- Consider letting a property before purchase. There are often good deal to be found once you are local that you may not have access to from afar.

Chapter 2

Residency

Visas

A visa is a document which allows non-citizens to enter, pass through, remain or exit a country. This clearance is only given once a specific set of circumstance has been verified. Before commencing the visa application process, you will have to consider what type of visa is best suited to your needs. There are many types of visas and each will have its own specific set of criteria which must be met in order to be granted. Take heart, though, that this is not a test. Countries around the world are keen to grant visas to those who offer valuable skills that are in short supply within their own country. While they may have slightly different labels, all visas tend to fall into one of the following categories.

Skilled workers

It is always best to have secured employment before applying for a visa, however, if your occupation is listed on your country's priority occupation list, then you will be eligible for migration without having a job offer. Certain countries will only offer temporary work visas initially; however, others, such as Canada, will offer permanent residence immediately to those with education, work experience and knowledge of English or French.

Unskilled workers

In certain places, such as Alberta, Canada, the need for unskilled labour outstrips supply. This is frequently in retail or tourism sectors. Experienced workers are in such high demand that the wages are frequently set at twice or

'Before commencing the visa application process, you will have to consider what type of visa is best suited to your needs.'

higher than average rates of pay. These positions tend to be very location specific. However, once you are local and have some national experience on your CV, you will find it easier to find employment in a new location if that is your desire.

Investors

Many countries grant a limited number of visas to individuals who will start a new commercial enterprise. New commercial enterprises are required to begin with the aim of creating employment for a minimum number of individuals. Often these visas will expect an initial sum as an investment in the local economy.

In the United States, Congress made the decision under the 1990 Immigration Act to allow up to 10,000 visas each year to be granted to investors. Each investor must invest a minimum of $500,000 in a target area or $1,000,000 elsewhere. Investors must also prove that they will create employment for 10 people. Different countries have their own unique targets set for recruiting investors. If you have the capital and the drive, it might be an exciting challenge to pursue.

Family sponsorship

This type of visa is for those who would like to take a spouse or dependents with them. Most countries are very obliging when it comes to keeping relations together, and once one family member has secured a job offer, the rest of the family will be entitled to visas. In many cases, dependent visas restrict employment entitlement. If you are emigrating with a spouse and you wish to be able to seek employment at a later date, it is important to take note of any restrictions.

Refugees and asylum seekers

Those who fear persecution due to their race, religion, nationality, political opinions, or for belonging to a specific social group may be able to apply for asylum or refugee status. If you are granted a visa as a refugee or asylum seeker, you may not be entitled to apply for benefits or government aid; however, in almost every country, you are permitted to apply for legal aid should you run into any problems with your immigration status.

While a visa tends to be thought of as simply a means of entering a country, there are certain countries which require foreign travellers to possess an exit visa before they will be permitted to depart. Each individual country will have a list of specific visas which they will grant. This varies from the dizzying array of visas for those entering the United States to the tidy little set of visas which are offered by New Zealand. There is little difference between the two. The names and specifics of each visa is simply a way for each country to monitor and encourage the right people to come to their country. The reality is there are two distinct categories of visa.

Nonimmigrant visas

Each country benefits greatly by receiving international visitors. Those who come to study, work or play enrich the culture, economy and education. Nonimmigrant visas tend to be less expensive and are relatively easy to acquire. The duration for nonimmigrant visas tends to range between 3 months and 2 years in length. For some, such as students or spouses, acquiring a nonimmigrant visa is the first step before applying for more permanent immigration status at a later date. Regardless of the type of visa, it is important to apply for your visa in advance. Most visas can only be granted while you are outside of your destination country. Locations such as the United Arab Emirates are an exception, and issue visas at their border.

'The names and specifics of each visa is simply a way for each country to monitor and encourage the right people to come to their country.'

Immigrant visas

Immigrant visas are more involved and generally are only accessible to those with a certain connection to the country. If you have a parent or spouse who already has citizenship, then you may be able to apply directly.

Do not worry if you do not have direct connections to your destination country. Once you have applied for a nonimmigrant visa, and have moved to your chosen destination, you will make the employment and country specific requirements which will allow you to apply for permanent immigration in the future.

If you are asked, and it is highly likely you will be asked, to provide a reason as to why you wish to enter a country, you could do worse than to rely on flattery. Take the time to research the country you are choosing, and to consider what it is that draws you to the place. If a relaxed lifestyle, greater employment opportunity and a language you are passionate about learning are a few of your reasons for going, then tell them.

In some countries, there are established residency programmes such as the Skilled Migration programme in Australia. This is designed to grant permanent residency to a limited number of people who are highly skilled in their field and are also deemed suitable by a number of other factors. It is not unusual for age to be taken in to account. The Australian Skilled Migration programme will only accept individuals between 18 and 44 years of age.

Are there any reasons that my application for a visa may be rejected?

Yes, unfortunately, there are many reasons that a visa may be rejected, including the following:

- You have a criminal record.
- You are considered to be a threat to national security.
- You have fraudulently misrepresented yourself on your application
- You are unable to prove strong ties to your country of origin.
- You have no legitimate reason for emigrating.
- You do not have any means of sustaining yourself.
- You have poor moral character.
- You are applying too close to the date of departure.

- You are a citizen of a country that is currently considered hostile by your destination country.
- You have previously visited or been a resident of a country which is considered hostile to your destination country.
- You have a communicable disease, such as tuberculosis.
- You have previously violated the laws of immigration or a visa.
- Your passport will expire soon or is already expired.

Citizenship

If attaining citizenship is your goal, it is worth noting that it is a long process. It is one that is very rewarding, but one that tends to be completed in stages. Those who have a spouse or parent who already holds citizenship tend to be eligible for citizenship more quickly. Nonetheless, many countries require you to have a sponsor, and there are frequently citizenship tests. These are both easily surmountable. If you are employed, then your employer would be an ideal sponsor. Citizenship tests will require you to gather and learn all sorts of interesting facts about the culture and history of the country in which you are naturalising.

There are a few countries that will not allow you to maintain two nationalities. It is worth considering this ahead of pursuing full citizenship. Most countries will require you to have attained a permanent leave to remain or indefinite right of abode before applying for citizenship. Depending on your unique circumstance this may be enough for you to live and work comfortably without having complete citizenship.

'If attaining citizenship is your goal, it is worth noting that it is a long process.'

Getting permanent residence

Generally, skilled workers and professionals will find that they are easily granted permanent residence. It is important to make the effort to learn the native language. Most countries expect those seeking permanent residence to be fluent in their national language. This is of course superfluous if you are emigrating to a country such as Canada or Australia.

Privileges for different nationalities

As a British citizen, you are entitled to travel freely through all EU member countries. Anyone who is a citizen of a country which belongs to the EU is automatically an EU citizen. You may settle anywhere within its territory without requiring advance permission from the local government. Once you have moved, you will be encouraged to apply for a national identity card. There are many benefits to having this card and it will provide an alternate proof of identity when travelling. There are many countries in Europe which a British passport holder may enter without a visa for up to 6 months. However, in many cases you may not have recourse to public funds and healthcare, and you may have work restrictions placed upon you. It is very important to research the requirements your destination will require. Unfortunately, being allowed to enter and remain, may not mean you are allowed the same rights as other national citizens.

'The cost of your visa is determined by how much it costs to process the application.'

Within the EU, there is a zone called the Schengen Area. This area is made up of 26 European countries which have nullified passport and immigration controls around their common borders. Britain did not sign the Schengen Agreement. However, should your route take you through one country and into another, you may not be subject to border controls. Equally, should you emigrate to a country which has signed the Schengen Agreement, you may wish to visit other countries with the freedom of such relaxed immigration rules.

Costs

The cost of your visa is determined by how much it costs to process the application. Unfortunately, the price of visas varies dramatically from country to country. Visas differ in their duration, and the entitlements they allow. Both of these factors may play a role in price of a given visa.

Price of a standard work visa

- £90 USA
- £215 Australia
- £97 Canada

- £105 New Zealand
- Approximately £35 for a Dubai work visa

Overcoming common difficulties

It is important to play by the rules in the emigration process. Many places, such as Spain, are really testy about illegal immigrants. If you are expelled as an illegal alien, you may be prevented from ever being able to live there. It is highly unlikely that an exception will be made on your behalf. Hence, it is always best to follow the immigration procedure carefully.

When you apply for a visa it is common for there to be an interview and criminal record check. It is very important to answer every question truthfully. If you are found to have misrepresented yourself, you may find yourself facing serious consequences.

Once you enter a country with the aim of applying for permanent residence, or with a view towards achieving citizenship, you will need to keep your visits to other countries short. While it varies, the general guideline is to keep absences to less than 12 weeks in duration. Most countries will revoke your residency rights if you leave the country for a prolonged duration.

Other problems commonly arise from applying for the wrong visa. Contact the national border agency to ensure the visa you are applying for will grant you all the abilities and entitlements that you will want. If you apply for a student visa which restricts the number of hours you can work, it may cause you difficulties later on when you are offered a placement with a local company.

Summing Up

- There are many types of visa, and it is important for you to be awarded a visa which entitles you to live and work in a manner that is suitable to your situation.

- If you initially apply for a nonimmigrant visa, it does not mean that you will not be eligible for citizenship at a later date. A nonimmigrant visa is an excellent way of securing vital connections with your new country.

- Make sure your passport is newly renewed before applying for a visa.

- As a British citizen, you are automatically a citizen of the European Union. This means that you can settle anywhere within its territory without requesting permission.

- In general, work visas are both affordable and renewable.

- Always remain completely honest through every stage of your application.

Chapter 3

Employment

Finding and then securing employment is the first major hurdle anyone considering emigration will face. Once you have a job offer, the rest of the journey is relatively smooth sailing. It is generally advised that you should start your job search as much as a year in advance of your intended leave date. You will need to consider the commencement dates and seasonal availability of certain employment sectors.

Once you have found an area of the job market that requires your skills, you will need to refine you CV to suit the specific needs of the employer you wish to contact. For example, in North America, résumés are used instead of CVs. These require a slightly different approach. The Internet is laden with useful templates and helpful websites to guide you through the process of all manner of job applications.

One of the most frustrating aspects of changing employers and countries can be that you may have to begin again at the bottom of your career ladder, regardless of the seniority you had achieved in the UK. Take heart, though, that once you show your new employer that you have the skills and have gained a little experience in your new country that you will quickly receive promotions.

When you begin your search for employment it will be worth your while to be flexible on your exact location. Once you are in a country it is relatively easy to change locations at a later date. Though you may find an area you had never previously considered is actually the place you had always hoped to find.

Certain parts of Canada have vastly different employment availability. Along the west coast in British Columbia seasonal workers and construction are the two major industries which are desperate for employees. In Alberta, the demand for unskilled retail and restaurant employees is so high that the hourly rates of pay stand at over twice the national average. The province's rapid expansion has led to emigrants being needed in farming, mining and education sectors.

'Finding and then securing employment is the first major hurdle anyone considering emigration will face. It is generally advised that you should start your job search as much as a year in advance of your intended leave date.'

Ontario remains a very popular emigration destination for Expats. However, the employment opportunities available in Ontario are primarily focused on professionals with significant previous experience.

Finding a job

There are many agencies that will offer to help you find a job and apply for a visa for a fee. There are no statistics available to rate their performance, but these agencies are one available route towards finding a job.

'Each country maintains a list of eligible occupations, and they will be specifically looking for applicants who are capable of filling a position which is on the list.'.

There are many ways of finding job opportunities on your own. You can search online where you will find many sites devoted to listing job opportunities specifically for those wishing to emigrate. Equally, you can browse sites which focus on listing jobs in their local area. As an EU citizen, you can use job centres abroad, and may even be eligible for jobseeker's allowance while you are searching for employment in a new country. EURES is a mobility portal which is run by the European Commission and is designed to allow you to view employment opportunities across Europe.

Newspapers and employment listings magazines are common places to find employment opportunities. Some of these publications list their advertisements online. While others may require a subscription, almost all publications are happy to post them abroad.

It never hurts to contact the major employers in your field directly. Even if they are not currently advertising, it may be worth a phone call or submitting a specially tailored CV to the correct department. Many of the larger companies will provide some compensation towards relocating, and if they are keen to take you on, they are known for paying for the costs of your visa and any retraining you may require.

Employment regulations

Each country has its own specific set of regulations, however, there are several which will be standard regardless of your choice of country. Each country maintains a list of eligible occupations, and they will be specifically looking for applicants who are capable of filling a position which is on the list. All prospective applicants are subject to minimum language threshold tests. It may be that you are not requested to take a language test, but you need to be prepared to do so. Employment Credential Assessments are becoming more regular and more heavily regulated. It is important to have all your original documents and transcripts in advance of applying for any employment position or visa. The application you fill out may not initially request a copy of your documents, but there are many cases where a request will be made to see original documents immediately after the application has been received, and if you cannot supply them immediately, your application will be rejected.

Some countries regulate employment through tick box style tests. Others operate on a points system. These systems were not created with the intention of working against you, but to ensure that the long-term prospects for both the country and the new migrants is successful.

Short-term work

If you are offered short-term work, it may mean that you are ineligible for a settlement visa. This may complicate the process of emigration, however, if you are able to show another tie to the country, such as having a spouse who will be in full-time employment, then you may be entitled to a permanent work visa. Working holiday visas are available for up to two years in length and offer quite generous conditions, should you prefer to take on a short contract.

Many people take the opportunity of a short-term work offer and use it as a chance to try out the area and lifestyle without having to completely sever their ties with the UK. This can also work to your advance if you wish to use the time to look for more permanent work opportunities and search for a new home. While you are in the country, you will be gain valuable in-country experience. Your short-term employer will also be able to provide you with a local reference, which may make the difference in whom your future employer chooses for the next available position.

'Many people take the opportunity of a short-term work offer and use it as a chance to try out the area and lifestyle without having to completely sever their ties with the UK.'

Permanent work

Securing a permanent position is the most common route to emigration. It is not unusual for permanent work positions to be offered on a contractual basis of one or two years. These contracts are typically renewable at the end of each term, and this should not affect your ability to apply for permanent residence.

Working culture and etiquette

First impressions count for a lot, and it is said customers buy the person not the product when they are doing business. For better or worse, this is ultimately true, and it is worth taking notes on how the most successful people within your new country behave. In certain cultures, such as Dubai, the etiquette is radically different. So much so, that you can buy books helping to navigate you through common pitfalls.

However, in places like Canada or the United States, the differences are more subtle. North Americans have a very 'work hard, play hard' attitude. There are significantly shorter holiday allowances, and as such days off work are used enthusiastically. Equally, the process of being hired may only take a matter of hours. It is not unusual for an employer to ask when a potential employee is willing to start work. The correct answer is 'today'.

In Australia, direct communication is expected, and punctuality is important. Humility will carry you further than drawing attention to achievements and academics as this tends to create a general mistrust. The bells and whistles sales pitch simply does not work in Australia, and there is little appreciation for high-pressure sales techniques.

Etiquette in New Zealand requires that you demonstrate what you can bring to a company and community, and to avoid trying to haggle or bargain. The business culture focuses on taking a direct and honest approach without any fluff.

Starting and running a business

The dream of running your own business and being your own boss is enticing, and it is all the more when you picture yourself doing so in your favourite location. Whether you dream of opening a bed and breakfast in France or perhaps you want to launch your current business abroad, there are several considerations to make in advance.

Since the global financial crisis, it is tougher than ever to access funding for small business start-up abroad. Governments welcome international investors, but for those without a sizable start-up sum it may seem daunting. That is not to say it cannot be done. By doing your research into the needs and competition in your destination country, you may find yourself eligible for more assistance than you initially expected. If you are able to create jobs, and can show that your business will support the local economy, you may find there are grants and tax breaks available.

The market for buying and selling small businesses is on the rise. While there are legal obstacles to overcome, such as licensing, you will find the process is occasionally less paperwork-intensive than it would be to run the same company within the UK.

Retirement

Before you depart, you will need to fill out a P85 form to inform the tax office that you are no longer a UK resident. Once you have sold your home, it is important to contact all utility and official agencies to ensure they are aware that you no longer own your home. If you choose to let out your property, then you will need to pay tax on the income received.

If you choose to retire abroad, you will still be entitled to receive any UK pension you already hold. Though it is worth noting, you may not receive yearly increases to your pension if you move outside of the European Economic Area. Also, it is worth checking that the pension age of your destination country will still recognise you as a pensioner as these limits vary.

'If you choose to retire abroad, you will still be entitled to receive any UK pension you already hold.'

Healthcare becomes increasingly important as we age. In some countries, you may be required to maintain private healthcare. While this will ensure you have excellent treatment, it can be expensive. However, if you are retiring within the EU, then you will only have to fill out an E121 form to prove your eligibility for national healthcare.

Once you have moved, you will need to consider how your estate will be handled should you die. You will need a new will which complies with local laws; however, if you still own property in the UK you will need to have a UK will. Each country has its own inheritance laws, and in order to be sure that your wishes are respected it is necessary to have your will written by an approved legal solicitor. There are many commercial will writing services who will offer to provide you with a will for a small fee. Many of these companies are not legally trained, and the will you receive may not correctly convey your wishes. The result will be that your family will then have to pay a solicitor to rectify the mistakes made, which can be costly. It is very important when you have a potentially complicated estate that involves international affairs to ensure your will is carefully drawn up by a professional.

Summing Up

- It is worth reformatting your CV to local preferences in order to give yourself the best possible representation.

- You may have to take a temporary demotion with your new company until you have gained national experience.

- It may be necessary to remain flexible on the exact area you move to as employment availability may be restricted to specific locations. This is just the beginning of your new life and may not be where you remain long term.

- Employment opportunities across the whole of Europe are available for everyone to view on the EURES website.

- Employers will expect you to be able to pass a minimum language threshold and to be able to present any original documents as proof of your qualifications.

- Short-term work contracts can be an excellent opportunity to try out a new country without making a commitment.

- Communication and culturally sensitive etiquette will make all the difference in performing well through job interviews.

Chapter 4

Property

Renting

Renting is a great way to explore a new area without the commitment of having purchased a property. Most rental properties have very similar deposit and rent payment plans to what you will find in the UK. In certain areas, it is common for landlords to rent properties through agents and in other areas, properties are almost exclusively rented privately.

The majority of properties will be let unfurnished. This can be both a blessing and a hindrance. Generally, it is just as easy to pick up bargain used furniture in most parts of the world as it is in the UK. Though transporting them home is not easy if you have not yet acquired a vehicle. However, when you have your own furniture, you do not have to worry over every little spill or scuff.

Unless your tenancy agreement states otherwise, you will be responsible for all utility and council tax bills. In France, you must give three months' notice before vacating the property, and your notice must be sent by registered post. Most countries have quirky little rules that need to be adhered to. These are not always obvious. It is worth either buying a book on tenancy law, or contacting your local council to request advice regarding your rights as a tenant. It is important that you know your rights and responsibilities to protect yourself from potential legal disputes or problem landlords. Usually it is easier to prevent a problem than it is to fix it.

Finding properties for sale

There are lots of websites dedicated to the booming market of British buyers who would like to purchase a property abroad. If you have a specific location in mind then a quick Internet search will quickly reveal the local estate agents.

Most will happily send you a complete list of properties. You may find it useful to leave your details and the type of property you are looking for with the estate agent so that they can send you information on future properties which fit your requirements as they come on the market.

That said, you may wish to leave your search open. Perhaps the property you buy will be one that requires a little more care and attention but is worth it in the end. There tends to be a season for house sales. This will vary depending on the location, but timing your search with the beginning of the house-selling season will ensure you are able to view the widest selection of properties.

There are properties which may be privately sold on a website or through newspapers. Even more so than at home, it is always best to employ a professional to go over your contracts and to have the property thoroughly investigated before parting with any money.

Important procedures

If you are not a naturalised citizen, then you may not immediately be entitled to buy a property. Many governments have chosen to regulate the properties sold to foreign buyers. You may have to submit an application to a review board before you will be granted the legal right to purchase property. If you are purchasing a property with the purpose of having a primary place of residence, then you are not likely to encounter any problems. If you want to buy a second home or a buy to let property, you will have to prove that your purchase of a property has a long-term benefit to the community. Once you are granted permanent residence, buying a property will become relatively straight forward.

Financial aspects

Not too long ago, owning a house abroad whether for use as a holiday house, home, or an investment, was a dream only realised by those with a lot of money to spare. Cheap travel and rising house prices have led to more than one million British people owning a second home in France and Spain alone. High street mortgage lenders offer competitive overseas mortgages, although, for some of the newly emerging countries such as Croatia, you may need to contact a specialist lender.

If you are considering buying a property within the EU, you may want to consider a euro mortgage. The euro mortgage often works out cheaper in comparison to UK high street mortgages, so long as you keep an eye on exchange rates. Euro mortgages are typically offered between 60-80%.

The reality is that in order to buy property abroad you will have to find around 20% of the purchase price. There are many ways you may choose to take advantage of in the pursuit of building an initial lump sum. Your savings are the first best option to consider. If you have the savings to buy a property outright, then there is little reason to do otherwise. Be careful of withdrawal time constraints and penalties. Many sellers are willing to be flexible for cash buyers if they receive adequate communication about any delays due to banking.

If you currently own your own home, you may choose to remortgage or take out an advance. An advance will increase the size of your mortgage. Occasionally, it is a good idea to remortgage. A new lender may offer you a better deal and a larger mortgage. This will allow you to cover the cost of both houses.

Equity release can be another financial solution. One type of equity release involves taking out a loan against your property. This is called a lifetime mortgage and is dependent upon your age. The interest on this loan accumulates over your lifetime. There will be no repayments to be paid during your life. Instead, the money owed is repaid after your death through the sale of the house.

Should you be paying into a personal pension fund, you could choose to withdraw up to 25% of it to raise capital.

Secured loans are relatively easy to acquire, and these will allow you to borrow a large sum which will have a long repayment period. Secured loans are only available to those who already own a property.

Any endowment policies you hold that are over 7 years old and are worth more than £15,000, can be surrendered or sold. While surrendering a policy will incur a penalty, selling a policy to an investor can be quite lucrative.

In the current climate, many people are struggling to get a foothold on the property ladder, and as such, co-ownership is becoming increasingly popular. If you have family or close friends with similar dreams and ambitions, perhaps

'If you are considering buying a property within the EU, you may want to consider a euro mortgage.'

this may allow both parties to generate enough income to purchase a suitable property. Of course, it is important to have a formal agreement drawn up to prevent future arguments or misunderstandings.

If you already have a lump sum but are concerned about making ends meet in your new home, then letting out your current property can be easily managed with a letting agent.

Regardless of what country you are in it is important to enquire in advance about sales taxes and estate agent fees. Each country will have its own version of the UK stamp duty, with places like Italy making the UK look positively affordable with its 10% combined property taxes which are charged in respect of the purchase price.

'Regardless of what country you are in it is important to enquire in advance about sales taxes and estate agent fees.'

Building your own home

For some, buying a plot of land and building a property is a dream worth overcoming a few challenges to achieve. Careful planning and a good solicitor will ensure that the purchase goes smoothly. Once you have purchased your land, you will need to find a reputable architect or surveyor who will design the property to your specifications. Don't work with anyone who is not up to date on the latest changes to regulations and laws, and always look into the supply of utilities. It can happen that due to a certain regulations electricity cannot be supplied, or that there is an issue with supplying water. Otherwise, you will have to go back and spend more to re-work your plans. Good contractors are best found by personal recommendation. The best of whom will be very busy. As such, you may not be able to start immediately. Finding a good project manager can take a lot of burden off your shoulders, especially if you are still based in the UK. Once your home is complete there may be further legal duties you must complete. Check with your solicitor to ensure that there are no nasty surprises.

Making money from your property

Buying property as an investment is an age-old tradition. It is possible to make large returns on properties if you are savvy and know what you are doing. There are professional agencies that specialise in up-and-coming markets.

They promise to sell you property at a low price with the promise of rising inflation that will make you rich. Perhaps this works for some, however, going into buying a property based on the idea that it will earn you money is risky. If the area becomes saturated, experiences bad weather, or perhaps has a change of government, property prices may plummet. In order to make money off a property, you need to do your research. There is a market for holiday lets, and for those of you who already have experience buying a property to fix up and sell on can be a very lucrative way to make a profit.

Selling a property abroad

When the time comes that you wish to sell your property, there will be several things to consider. First, you will want to have your property valued. Then you will have to decide to sell your property. You may choose to sell through an estate agent, an auction, or sell the property privately. An estate agent should work hard to get the very best price for you. However, they do tend to come at a cost. In France, you may be required to pay as much as 12% of the property price in estate agent fees. If you decide to go ahead with trying to sell your property privately, research exactly what you as a seller are required to do to ensure you do not fall short of the law. In Australia, selling your property privately is the popular choice. This is in part due to how easy it is to list a property online, and due to many people refusing to pay the ever-increasing agent fees.

Top ten tips when buying a property abroad

1. Never put a deposit down the same day you view a property. Allow yourself a reflection period to avoid buyer's remorse.

2. Open a bank account in your new country and set up standing orders for your bills and taxes. In countries such as France, Portugal and Spain, failure to pay your taxes on time can lead to court proceedings and even the seizure of your property.

3. Before making a purchase you need to have an independent valuation carried out. This will bring any wiring, damp or subsidence issues to your attention and should expose any boundary disputes.

4. Consult independent solicitors, architects and surveyors before considering a purchase.

5. Do not sign a contract you do not understand, especially one that is written in a foreign language.

6. Ideally, try to arrange your mortgage in the same currency that you receive your salary.

7. Ask your solicitor to look for debts on the property. It is all too easy to inherit someone else's headache.

8. Request an opt-out clause to be written into your contract if you are in the process of arranging finances. This way, if your loan is not agreed, then you should have your deposit returned.

9. Remember to budget for the costs beyond the asking price. There will be taxes, insurance, legal fees, and more.

10. Don't hesitate to contact the authorities to enquire about the lawfulness of the charges you are being asked to pay. Not everyone is honest, and if you are in doubt, ask the local authorities.

'Do not sign a contract you do not understand, especially one that is written in a foreign language.'

Summing Up

- If you are renting your property, it is in your best interests to learn the local tenancy law. It is easier to avoid problems than it is to fix them.

- Most estate agents prefer to be contacted by email. It is less expensive to send a PDF of the available properties by email, than it is to print and post it.

- Generally, emigrants are allowed to purchase a property with the intent of living in the property. The laws are not always eager to permit emigrants to purchase properties with the intent of leasing them to another person.

- You will need at least 20% of the purchase price, regardless of where your mortgage comes from.

- The best contractors are found by personal recommendation. Business directories do not check for qualifications and as such should not be blindly trusted.

- Never sign a contract you are unable to read and understand.

- Always ask questions if you are unsure about any aspect of purchasing or selling your property.

Chapter 5

Finances

Embassies and consulates

Embassies and consulates have come about as a way of governments trying to represent their citizens in foreign countries.

Embassies are described as a permanent diplomatic mission and tend to be located in capital cities. An ambassador comes from a prestigious level of government and is the highest official within an embassy. They are responsible for representing their home country and taking care of major diplomatic issues.

In member countries of the Commonwealth nations, the office of High Commissioner is used, as these countries do not exchange ambassadors.

Consulates are smaller than embassies and handle minor diplomatic issues, such as issuing visas and caring for tourists and expatriates. Typically, if you require the assistance of your government while you are abroad, you should find a consulate who will help you with anything from trade relationships to migration.

'Consulates are smaller than embassies and handle minor diplomatic issues, such as issuing visas and caring for tourists and expatriates.'

Banking abroad

Many of the high street banks have services specifically tailored to Expats living abroad. Barclays and HSBC offer a wide range of services from cheap money transfers to multinational accounts. They may also be able to advise you about financial planning. Barclays recommends numerous ways to save money, from advising about your right to continue paying into your ISA despite not being a UK resident, through to the tax-related issues that occur for different kinds of investments within different jurisdictions.

Despite how convenient it may seem to switch accounts with your current bank, you will probably want to open a bank account in your new country of residence.

In certain business or legal circumstances, you will probably be asked to supply banking details to prove your credibility. When your bank's address is overseas it will not appear as though you are settled for a long stay. Equally, in many foreign countries cheques are still common, and cards are infrequently used. You will need cheques which are in the local language and currency. It would not be unusual for anyone to reject a cheque that was not only from a foreign bank, but also in a currency they do not recognise. When the time comes that you would like to apply for a loan, you will also find that your old bank is significantly less generous to someone with a foreign address.

While most people are reluctant to change their banks, it is a relatively painless process. Just go into the bank of your choice and make an appointment to speak with someone. It is likely that you will have to provide proof of everything from marriage certificates, birth certificates, a passport and utility bills. In Canada and the United States, the banks do vary a great deal. It is worth shopping around for the best account for your purposes. In many other countries banking is not a right but a privilege that has to be paid for. It is likely that every cash withdrawal and cheque that you use will generate a small charge. To avoid ending up with an ugly monthly bill, it is important to ensure you have taken out the best account to suit your lifestyle needs, and then to budget your withdrawals.

Online banking is another UK standard option that is not available as readily. Unfortunately, even when online banking is available, you may find there is a charge for using this service, as well.

When banking abroad it is important to keep a close eye on your balance. In the UK, if you should write a cheque for a little more than what your account contains, your bank will probably cash it, and you may receive a small charge for the interest, or you may receive a letter in the post asking you to be more careful. Most overseas banks do not share this gentle approach to their customers. Instead, they tend to charge a significant fine on top of not cashing your cheque. In certain countries, it is simply illegal, and your bank must sign your name onto a national database which records anyone who has written a faulty cheque. Once your name is on this database it is unlikely that anyone will take a cheque from you again.

Cost of living

As British prices continue to rise, it is appealing to consider moving abroad, where you may hope to find a lower cost of living. The difficulty with assessing the cost of living in any country is due to the vast regional differences. In Britain, you may find very affordable houses in rural Scotland, which could not be compared to housing in London. The price differences between the everyday costs of living in different areas will vary dramatically according to the difference in lifestyle, as well. It will be important to research the exact area you are considering before finalising your predicted expenditure. In the Canadian prairies, you can purchase land for as little as a dollar an acre. Meanwhile, properties in major cities are priced competitively with most major cities around the globe.

Spain is a popular destination for British emigrants due to the potential for an affordable lifestyle. Basics, such as eating in restaurants and buying staple groceries, are cheaper in comparison with the average costs in the UK. Leisure costs and household expenses tend to be inexpensive in comparison to the UK average. However, property prices are extremely variable.

Canada is another country which is favoured for its lower cost of living. This may not be the case in all aspects. In Western Canada, hydroelectricity provides inexpensive electricity. In other regions utilities can be significantly more expensive than UK households, not to mention the very cold winters which will add further strain to household running costs. Transport costs such as petrol do tend to be slightly less expensive, however, the average person will travel significantly further between destinations which tends to average out the differences in price.

Australia's cost of living is very similar to Britain. In general, the daily household expenses, property prices and transportation costs are all similar to average prices in Britain. Groceries tend to be slightly more expensive than they are in the UK, however, the average gross disposable income in Australia for the year 2011 was £27,790, whereas the average gross disposable income in the UK

'Spain is a popular destination for British emigrants due to the potential for an affordable lifestyle.'

was £21,326. If you are working and earning your income domestically while living in Australia, then it is very likely that your standard of living will be improved. For those that are drawing an income from a pension or British investments, you are going to find that your general cost of living is about the same.

Taxation

Each country has its own individual tax rules. It is important to be aware of the new rules and to contact the appropriate authorities in your new country. Many countries have a Double Taxation treaty with the UK. This mean that if you are earning an income in one country and living in another then you will not be expected to pay taxes in both countries.

Do I have to tell tax office I am leaving?

'Each country has its own individual tax rules.'

Actually, you do not have to inform the tax office. Many people leave the country and do not inform the authorities. The primary reason that most people do not inform the tax office of their departure is that most fear dealing with endless forms and a large headache.

Why should I contact my local tax office?

If you take the time to contact your local tax office before departure, your interests will be protected. By leaving the country officially, you will be able to return to Britain on good terms. Once you have notified the tax office that you are a non-resident of Britain, all future personal mail will be removed from being posted to your previous address. Another underestimated reason for notifying your tax office of your departure is that many people are eligible for a sizable tax rebate. As taxes are calculated on an annual estimated salary, anyone who leaves part of the way through a tax year will probably have overpaid and be eligible for a refund.

How do I inform the correct authorities?

If you do not have an accountant, then the primary form you need to fill out is the P85. This is the form which will allow you to stop future tax returns and will allow you to apply for any tax rebates that you are owed. This form is available from your local tax office, or you can download the form online from the HMRC website (see the help list). The P85 form isn't difficult to complete and shouldn't require more than 15 minutes to fill out. You will need to submit your P45 and date of departure with your submission.

If you are unsure where your local tax office is located, you will be able to find the correct office by looking at your P45 or P60. There should be three digits under the PAYE reference field which will correspond to your tax office number. If you go online to the HMRC website, you will be able to enter these three digits and HMRC will supply you with the correct address.

Unfortunately, tax offices are not always quick to return forms. Therefore it is recommended that you submit your forms three months before your departure.

'Health insurance is important in most countries outside the UK and should be a priority.'

What if I am self-employed?

For those who are self-employed, it is very important to maintain good communication with your tax office. You may be fined if you do not file your Self Assessment forms due to not having informed the authorities that you are no longer in the UK. If you are self-employed, you will still be required to submit a P85 form. It is very likely that you will also be required to submit Self Assessment tax returns for the first few months after you have emigrated. If you are continuing to trade in the UK, you will have to contact your local tax office to discuss your individual tax requirements.

Insurance

Based on your destination and lifestyle, you will have to consider what kind of insurance you will need. Health insurance is important in most countries outside the UK and should be a priority. Even if you are living in Europe where emergency healthcare is free, you will still need to protect yourself by purchasing health insurance.

Life insurance is another important consideration to make. There are several types of life insurance. Term insurance covers you for a specified period of time. The other type of life insurance is a whole life policy and will cover you until the end of your life. In some countries, premiums are set by a governing body, and in others the rates are set privately. It is always worth shopping around to ensure you receive the coverage that you want and need.

Property insurance for building, contents and liability is popular with many people due to the security it provides. While it is not mandatory in most countries, it is essential in Australia if you would like to be approved for a mortgage, and it is generally considered a wise investment. Before you sign an insurance policy, it is worth asking whether the policy covers contents on a 'new for old' basis. Take the time to ask your new provider about any queries you may have; from whether or not your building insurance covers the cost of rebuilding or the market value to annual premium increases. In Spain, the cost of rebuilding a house may be significantly more than its market value.

It is compulsory in most countries to have a minimum of third party insurance when driving. In certain countries, the policies for auto insurance may vary between regions. It will be important to ensure that you have adequate insurance before you drive, as in certain countries driving under insured can result in prosecution and even a prison sentence.

Summing Up

- If you require assistance with the reissuing of your visa or advice on your legal rights as an emigrant, then you should contact your local consulate.

- While you may remain a customer of your current bank, it will inevitably make your life easier if you switch your accounts over to a local bank.

- Always check your account balances before writing a cheque. Writing a cheque which you do not have the funds for is a greater offense in many countries than it is in Britain.

- It does not matter in which country you reside, there will always be expenses, and they will steadily increase. However, you may be better placed to earn more in another country while working in the same position you currently occupy. The difficulty is in finding the balance. Nonetheless, you will avoid difficulties if you plan your finances frugally.

- Once you have completed your P85, you will no longer be responsible to submit any further tax returns, and you may be eligible for a tax rebate.

- You will need to consider carefully what types of insurance you need in your new country.

Chapter 6

Education

Why study abroad?

Rising tuition fees and caps on the number of university places are just two of the reasons motivating aspiring students to look abroad. The increasingly demanding job market requires everyone to make an extra large effort to stand out from the crowd. Studying abroad may not only allow you to set yourself apart from your peers for your ingenuity and leadership qualities, but for the many communication skills you will develop and improve.

There are many good reasons to study abroad. If you have ever tried to learn a second language, you may have found it really quite difficult without practical application and motivation. Choosing to study abroad can provide you with the opportunity to learn a new language which will broaden your employment horizons and strengthen your global understanding.

Throughout your studies, you will have the opportunity to travel on your weekends, which will allow you to familiarise yourself with a new culture. Cultures differ on a far deeper level than just their cuisine, clothing and language. A country's unique culture represents the beliefs, values and perceptions that provide the building blocks of their civilisation. Taking the time to experience cultural difference will undoubtedly cause you to reflect on your own culture and your own personal beliefs. It will also help you to develop your understanding and ability to empathise with other cultures, which will improve not only your daily life but your ability to work more successfully with a wider range of people in your career.

While studying internationally, you will have the opportunity to befriend other international students who are studying abroad and this will increase the network of peers you have across the globe.

'Choosing to study abroad can provide you with the opportunity to learn a new language which will broaden your employment horizons and strengthen your global understanding.'

One aspect of studying in a foreign country that tends to surprise people, is how different studying may be. You may find a break in the monotony of your academic routine and trying develop new approaches to education improves your overall study experience.

Globalisation and increased economic interdependence have led to more and more countries around the world to try to encourage their students to study abroad. The competencies gained are invaluable in everything from improving communication in business negotiations to successfully building communities.

Applications

The general rule, which applies universally, is that you should begin to fill out your application earlier rather than later. Occasionally, you may need to take an additional test before your application can be processed. It is always in your best interests to ask for advice and guidance from a guidance counsellor at your university of choice. Students are often provided with a significant amount of advice and assistance when preparing their application that, as an international student, you will not have the benefit of unless you ask.

Asia

Asia is home to some of the most highly respected universities in the world. Universities will expect you to approach them directly and to apply through their specific application process. Course start dates vary a great deal, even within certain institutions, and as such it is important to start considering your options early.

Australia

Australia is an excellent place to study for more reasons than just its fantastic climate. The application process is relatively simple in comparison to that of the United States, though there are many well-reputed education agents who will assist you in everything from enrollment to housing and visas. There are no extra exams to take, and for international students there is no formal interview process, with the exception of medicine. The Australian university calendar starts in February and runs through until November, which allows students December and January for holiday time.

Canada

Canada offers a high standard of living and quality education at a significantly lower cost to international students than you will find in most parts of the world. Canadian campuses focus a lot of time and effort on community and lifestyle. The general philosophy is 'work hard, play hard'. As such, students will find that there are hundreds of clubs, sports teams and student organisations which hold an abundance of activities to enhance the university experience. If you are currently a student, or have completed part of a degree, Canadian institutions tend to be quite generous in their transfer credit policies which can be very helpful. Each university will need to be contacted individually as every university will have its own admission policy.

Europe

As a citizen of the EU, you should not have to pay any more in tuition fees than a national in that country. However, it is worth looking into the European Union Lifelong Learning Programme. There is a programme called Erasmus which offers financial support for students who plan to study abroad for more than 24 weeks. Many programmes offered in the EU are at a significantly lower tuition price to those offered in the UK. However, it is important to ensure that you can find your courses in a language within which you are familiar.

New Zealand

The New Zealand education system was modelled after the British system, which offers a relatively familiar educational route for UK students. The application process is straightforward; however, the degree requirements are less so. The degrees offered in New Zealand have familiar titles such as Bachelors, Masters and PhDs; however, the degree courses are far more flexible than they are in the UK. Students enter general degrees and choose a major. This allows individual students to customise their studies and provides the ability to choose additional electives to suit their personal preferences and abilities.

United States

The United States are a popular education destination with British students for many reasons. First their education system is tailored to suit individuals from all backgrounds. From Ivy league universities to polytechnical colleges. The United States admissions schedule is roughly the same as the UK. The United States do have slightly different requirements and require all applicants to take the Scholastic Aptitude Test, otherwise known as an SAT.

Funding

'Sourcing and securing funding for your studies can be daunting regardless of the country.'

Sourcing and securing funding for your studies can be daunting regardless of the country. Different countries will have different tuition fees, and individual ways of paying. Planning ahead and doing your research is the only way to be successful.

If you would like to study at an institution in Europe, then you should be allowed to pay fees as a national student. Even if you have to pay ghastly international student fees, there are many opportunities to get funding for your studies.

Each university will have funding available to potential students who qualify depending on their situation and abilities. It will be important for you to contact your financial advisor for international students. Their role is to help you access any funding you are eligible to receive. Don't be ashamed to make enquiries about what is available. There are many funding avenues which will not receive a single applicant for several years in a row due to their specific eligibility requirements, or simply because of lack of awareness. International tuition awards, fellowships, research grants, bursaries and scholarships are just a few of the types of funding typically offered at each university.

Outside of applying for funding from the university you are applying for, there are three other primary channels to explore. Only a few of the hundreds of possible options are listed under each channel.

Charities

- The Association of Commonwealth Universities is a UK-registered charity. Established in 1913, it is the oldest international university network. The ACU offers scholarships and bursaries for students who wish to study at institutions throughout the British Commonwealth.

- Doctoral students studying in the EU, should look into the Marie Curie scheme.

- Contact the local Rotary Foundation and ask for applications for funding for international academic study.

Government funding

- The Fulbright Commission offers funding to those who wish to study at an institution in the United States. The Commission was created to cultivate cultural understanding between the UK and the United States.

- National Science and Engineering Research Council invests in Canada's capabilities within the science and technology industries by providing research grants for both national and international students.

- The Australian government offers three funding awards for international students: Endeavor Awards, Australian Leadership Awards and Australian Development Scholarships.

Educational funding through industry

In most industries you will find that there is sponsorship available through major corporations. These tend to be available as grants and work placements, which may lead to further employment after your studies. Due to the nature of these opportunities, it will be important for you to familiarise yourself with the leading companies within your industry and to contact them directly.

Qualifications

Many qualifications are transferable. Nonetheless, many will require official recognition should you wish to work in a country other than the one in which you received your qualification. This tends not to be as complicated as it might sound. Once you have experience and a background you can usually practice temporarily while you wait for your qualifications to be recognised. It is always important to check to see if your profession is regulated as you will need to contact the proper association and register as a member.

Schooling and young children

If you are a parent, then emigrating can feel even more daunting. Just remember that children are resilient and have a great sense of adventure. If you approach your move with enthusiasm, they will soon pick it up too.

'Many qualifications are transferable.'

If you are emigrating to a country where the language is not your native tongue, you will have to decide whether or not you want your children to learn a second language and integrate into the local school system. In most cases, this happens far more quickly and painlessly than parents expect. Children under the age of eight years old will frequently be fluent in their new language in as little as six months. Older children do tend to struggle a little bit, but soon find themselves conversing and interacting as though they have always been capable of expressing themselves in a foreign language. It is not unusual for parents to be muddling through learning a new language long after their children have developed such a fluency that they may not choose to converse as frequently in English. This can be a concern for some, and it may be worth considering to take time to practise English at home on a certain day to keep skills sharp.

In many countries, schooling at the standard we expect in the UK is not free. This can be a shocking new cost for parents who are not expecting tuition fees. For some, they would prefer to ensure their children are continuing with their British education. This may be of particular importance if your child is midway through their A levels, or perhaps if you have concerns about the transferability of education available in the area in which you live. Many families choose to enroll their children in international schools. These schools will offer students the opportunity to achieve internationally-recognised qualifications like the international baccalaureate or British qualifications such as A levels. For families with such concerns, there are numerous Expat home education courses and resources available. Everything from online courses to complete lesson plans with tutoring support can offer the support required to ensure that your child can complete their education in line with the UK's national curriculum.

No matter which way you choose to go about it, the first few months will be the hardest, however, the benefits of new experiences and a second language are priceless. If you are moving to an area where there is an established expatriate community, then there is a good chance that there will be an experienced and supportive community who will be keen to help you through the transition.

'The benefits of new experiences and a second language are priceless.'

Summing Up

- Going abroad to study may broaden your employment opportunities and improve your CV.

- It is never too early to start your application. Many institutions take applicants up to two years before the course start date.

- Certain countries will require you to take further tests. In the United States, all students are expected to complete the Scholastic Aptitude Test.

- Funding is only made available to those who ask for it. There are lots of funding channels available to explore. Don't miss out and pay more than you have to.

- If you are part of a recognised profession, you will be required to register as a member of the professional association in your new country.

- There are lots of schooling options for school-age children. Whether you choose to enroll them in a local school, with the aim of your child learning a new language, or should you choose an international school in order to allow your child to achieve their British qualifications, there will be an option to suit your family's needs. Many parents will choose to combine standard schooling with home education to ensure all their child's educational needs are fully addressed.

Chapter 7

Culture

Culture shock

Initially, your move to a new country may feel like an extended holiday. For the first few weeks, you may feel elated as you explore your new environment and enjoy the rich new experiences. With so many interesting experiences to take part in and a new area to explore, you will be learning new information at an incredible rate. However, being in a new environment means your senses are constantly on alert. This is exhausting and can take a toll on your body and mind. There are many factors believed to cause culture shock, and sensory exhaustion is just one of them. It is believed that being in a new country where everything is different can lead to feeling as though your old life is no longer the accepted way of doing things. On top of this, frustration over the difficulty of learning how to perform what were once simple tasks, such as public transport or banking, can lead to feeling overwhelmed. Practical differences from adapting your gut flora to new bacterial levels and overcoming changes to your circadian rhythm take time to adjust to fully. Difficulty accessing favourite foods, or common medicines can fuel anxiety which may already be quite high due to communication differences.

What is culture shock?

This is the unpleasant feeling that you may experience when you are in a completely new surrounding. Culture shock is described as being a unique experience for each individual, and not everyone will experience culture shock.

Symptoms of culture shock you may experience inlcude:

- Anger

- Depression
- Sadness
- Loneliness
- Feelings of inadequacy
- Physical pain and discomfort
- Insomnia or excessive sleep
- Loss of identity
- Almost grief-like longing for family and friends
- Mood swings
- Change in appetite
- Feelings of hostility towards nationals

'It is important to allow yourself time to adjust to this massive change in your life.'

It is important to allow yourself time to adjust to this massive change in your life. Regular exercise and establishing a good support network will go a long way to helping you feel your best more quickly. A new hobby, taking up volunteering or joining a sports team may provide you something to focus on when you are feeling blue.

Do not feel guilty if you wish to seek out a community group which is made up of those from your native community. There are many benefits to socialising with others who are not only going through a similar transition, but will also be able to reminisce with you fondly about common experiences.

Socialising

Socialising is every bit as vital for adults as it is for children. By going out and socialising with other people in your new country, you will have the opportunity to discover and acquire social norms and customs. Socialising will improve your self-confidence and esteem, and should alleviate feeling lonely. According to studies from Bupa, regularly participating in social activities improves your mental functioning and can reduce the risk of Alzheimer's disease.

The actual act of walking into a completely new situation and interacting with strangers can be quite frightening. Especially so, when at first you are unfamiliar with the cultural linguistic faux pas and nuances, body language, and are not best placed to discern false friends from genuine ones. Nonetheless, the more you build your community and support network, the more settled and confident you will feel. If you can overcome the initial nerves and pursue social opportunities, you should find that your overall stress is reduced and that your general mood is improved.

Sports

Joining a gym or sports club will offer excellent opportunities to meet others with similar interests. It does not matter if your ability level in a certain sport is better than average. In general, local sports clubs are comprised of people who play for the exercise and enjoyment, not due to their exceptional skill level. While playing a sport you played in your home country may allow you to carry over a familiar pastime, you may decide you would like to try something new. Perhaps you have never taken a yoga class, tried martial arts or tennis. Now may be the perfect opportunity, and should you decide you do not enjoy the experience, you can always try something else.

'The more you build your community and support network, the more settled and confident you will feel.'

Evening classes

Local recreation centres, libraries, colleges and local shops are all places which may offer short courses throughout the year. Courses on all subjects of special interest can be found if you take the time to look. From local history and pottery to painting miniature models, there is something for everyone.

Religious groups

If you have a faith which is important to you, it may make a big difference to your transition to socialise and find support through others whom share your beliefs.

Pubs and clubs

You don't have to drink in order to go out and socialise. Pubs and clubs tend to be central hubs for local people to socialise. Many of these venues will cater to a particular set of interests, such as sports or jazz music. Calling in advance, to find out about any scheduled events, will allow you to find out more about the interests for which the venue caters and whether it would suit you.

Volunteer

Not only is it a great way to play a positive role in your new community, volunteering will provide you the opportunity to meet new people. There are many kinds of volunteering. If you do not feel ready to commit to a regular position then perhaps consider joining a group that provides one-off support within the community, such as cleaning up a local beach. Most charities will have an annual walk or run to raise money for their cause, this can be an excellent way to be involved in a project on a short-term basis.

Annual events are excellent opportunities to become involved in a community and to develop your history with a specific place. While it can be very difficult initially, time will pass quickly and you will soon feel more confident and achieve a sense of belonging.

Food and drink

One of the many concerns you may have about a radical change of location may be the cuisine. For some, moving abroad is an exciting new chapter in their diet and they look forward to embracing food created within a new culture.

For others, it may be a point of anxiety as they worry about having to forego their favourites from home. In many cases, you should be able to find a decent alternative on the shelves of your new grocery store. There is a general trend towards having certain aisles that are dedicated to international cuisine, and you are very likely to find many of your favourites there.

Another avenue to explore is the Internet, where you will find an abundance of shopping sites, which are dedicated to delivering old favourites to those living abroad. Even Amazon regularly carries items with free delivery to international customers.

Even your favourite fast food restaurants are very likely to be available. Domino's pizza has stores in over 70 countries, KFC serves customers in over 120 countries and Subway has locations in 102 countries. Many of the UK shops are willing to deliver internationally, and Amazon's online grocery section frequently offers discounts that rival the supermarkets.

Shopping

Countries differ dramatically in their approach to shopping. In many places, there is little demand for the vast amount of commercial goods we deem as normal in the UK, and as such they are in limited supply. Many places do not buy into fashion trends, and there is subsequently far fewer clothing stores and styles from which to choose. This can be a great way to save money as style trends are very slow to change, making frequent clothes purchasing an unusual pastime. Sewing your own clothes is very popular in many parts of the world and it may be a bit of a shock to find more fabric stores available than clothing shops.

Convenience foods are another common British household item that is not always available as widely overseas. Fast foods and street venders may be cheap and plentiful, but in most cases you will not find the large chiller cabinets of ready meals. In many overseas countries, food will be significantly cheaper than it is in Britain. However, it is very likely that the supermarkets will not carry out of season products due to high shipping costs. Buying direct from farmers or from the local market tends to be popular and significantly cheaper still than buying from the supermarket.

'In many overseas countries, food will be significantly cheaper than it is in Britain.'

Public holidays and events

It may take a while to adjust to the change in holidays and festivals in a new country. Many expatriates choose to celebrate the holidays with which they are familiar, regardless of the country in which they are living. For some, this is a reassuring way to maintain ties with their home country and their personal traditions. Most employers are relatively understanding regarding major holidays and are flexible about allowing foreign workers time to participate in their religious and cultural celebrations. Nonetheless, it may be initially disappointing to celebrate the winter holidays in the heat of New Zealand or Australia's summer months. It will certainly take time to readjust your expectations and create new traditions and routines.

There will inevitably be many national holidays and cultural customs which the locals will observe. At first you may feel awkward to participate, however by joining in you will not only show your willingness to embrace their culture, but may find you develop new and enjoyable celebration rituals, which ease the loss you may be feeling regarding changes to your own celebrations.

In certain parts of the world, public holidays and even Sundays may be marked as days where there is no trade. This is a lovely change of pace for most so long as you are aware of these dates and are able to prepare in advance. It is worth downloading a public holidays calendar for your destination country and keeping it to hand. Do not plan a house move, or any major changes over a long weekend in a foreign country. Unlike in the UK, where most shops open for a few hours and you can still access cash from an ATM machine, this is not the case in many other countries, and nobody will even answer their phone to offer you assistance. This may seem quite brutal, but it is simply a difference in priorities.

Politics

No matter in which country you choose to live, you will have to become familiar with the politics. For better or worse, each country has tried to find a system that will best serve its citizens. Many Commonwealth countries, such as Canada and Australia, were once under the direct rule of Britain. While they are both independent countries, their governments still retain many similarities to the British system. If you are moving to the United Arab Emirates, then you may find the governing system to be significantly different. It may take time to become familiar and comfortable with a new system of government. That is understandable. One of the best ways to overcome any concerns you may have is to learn as much as possible about your new country's local and national government structures. As soon as you are allowed you should register to vote. Being a citizen is an important responsibility and with that responsibility comes certain rights and privileges. By participating in the public voting process, you are contributing to your community. Voting is also an important part of integrating into a society.

'Being a citizen is an important responsibility and with that responsibility comes certain rights and privileges.'

Summing Up

- Once the initial excitement wears off, you may feel a little blue. This is not unusual, and you are not alone, should you experience 'culture shock'.

- Culture shock is experienced differently by each person. Symptoms can range from depression to physical pain.

- One of the most effective ways to beat culture shock is to get involved in your new community.

- Socialising is important for your self-confidence and to alleviate loneliness. Try finding an activity or group that practises one of your interests. This will help you motivate yourself to attend despite any nervous feelings.

- Exploring a new cuisine is an exciting opportunity to find new foods and expand your diet.

- If you can't find your favourite foods in your local supermarket, it is worth looking online for a dedicated expatriate shop.

- Convenience foods and clothing trends may not be readily available in your new location. While it may take some time to adjust, it is likely that you won't miss it for long.

- Each country will have its own cultural holidays. While these may be unfamiliar, why not try celebrating the local holidays? You can continue to celebrate your familiar holidays and traditions as well, and may find positive reception by inviting your new acquaintances to join you.

- Learning about the political system in your new country will enhance your understanding of the society in which you live and to make an informed decision once you are allowed to vote.

Need2Know

Chapter 8

Lifestyle

Moving with pets

Moving house with pets can be a challenge, but it is even more challenging when the move involves changing countries. Before you book your pet's plane tickets, you will need to investigate if your pet will be subject to quarantine.

Countries quarantine animals to reduce the spread of disease, primarily rabies. All the countries in the world have been divided up into three categories depending upon their incidence of rabies. The UK is a rabies-free country, so you should be able to travel with your pet to almost any country without restriction, provided you have the right import permit. However, it is worth considering if you will want to return to the UK at any time with your pet, because if your destination country is not on the rabies-free country list, then your pet will be subject to a blood titre test or quarantine on re-entry.

Most countries, including the European Union have a country specific health certificate. In countries where there is no national pet health certificate a veterinary certificate of health will be sufficient. Alongside your pet's passport, you should include an international health certificate, which needs to be completed by your vet within 21 days before the date of travel. As close as possible to the date of departure is preferred. Many countries will request that your pet's documents are available in their native language. Ask your vet to see if they are able to provide this service.

An International Health Certificate should contain the following information:

■ Pet's name

■ Age

■ Country of origin

'The UK is a rabies-free country, so you should be able to travel with your pet to almost any country without restriction, provided you have the right import permit.'

- Breed

- Colour

- Contact details for owner

- Statement of good health and that the pet is free from parasites

- Vaccine history

It may be necessary for your pet to have an additional rabies booster depending on the vaccine schedule in your destination country. Currently, the UK offers a three yearly booster; however, this is frequently not recognised, and your pet may require another booster regardless of when they received their last vaccine.

Most species of pet will be required to have a microchip ahead of departure, and the paperwork will need to be present with their health and travel documents.

The most common problems arise when an animal is taken abroad, and the health documents are incomplete and incorrectly filled out, or the necessary paperwork is not supplied.

Once you have sorted out all your pet's paperwork you can start to plan their travel. Each airline has its own set of rules. It is worth your peace of mind to shop around. Certain airlines will allow up to one pet per person to travel in the cabin area of the plane. This is obviously ideal from the perspective of knowing your pet is safe, warm and comfortable. However, many airlines only carry pets in the cargo. The cargo area where pets travel will be temperature controlled and pressurised. Nonetheless, do not hesitate to query anything that causes you concern. All animals travelling by plane will have to be securely contained inside a suitable pet travel container. Most airlines will ask that food and water dishes be secured to the inside of the travel container and for any paperwork or travel documents to be secured to the exterior of the travel container. The best way to secure your documents to your travel container is to put them inside a strong plastic envelope and duct tape it on to the container. Add a label, which states that the envelope contains original documents, and they are not to be removed. Make copies of all of your documents and keep these separately, just in case. If your travel container has wheels, it is advisable to remove these or have them fixed so that your pet will not be sliding around throughout their journey. Most airlines request that absorbent material or bedding is placed with the pet, and encourage comfort blankets and soft toys. It is best, however, not to take hard dog bones or animal by-products, such as dried pigs' ears. Should an episode of turbulence during your flight occur, a hard object could cause your pet an injury.

Languages

Roughly 160 countries have created measures to protect and support the use of their national language. This has led to laws being created which pertain to many aspects of daily life, from the languages that are allowed to be used in product descriptions and on packaging, to the necessary steps immigrants must take in the process of becoming citizens.

Not every country will insist you become fluent in their language, and many will use English frequently in their daily lives. However, there is a great deal to lose by never trying. Your entire experience changes from being an outsider looking in on a culture, to gradually becoming a part of it. It is incredibly difficult to connect with someone in your community when they do not make an effort to communicate or improve their ability to communicate with you. This is called assimilation. Assimilation is important for building social bonds in your new community. Long term, your employment prospects are vastly improved by being bilingual. Your own security is dependent upon your ability to understand your rights and the laws that protect you. Equally, should you require emergency assistance, or even be in need of directions, having the ability to communicate will make all the difference.

'Long term, your employment prospects are vastly improved by being bilingual.'

There are numerous ways to learn a new language, and by far the most successful is to jump straight in to an environment which allows you to practise. You may choose to take a course before you depart to give yourself a head start, or you may choose to wait and take courses directly in your destination country.

Both options have their merits. Taking courses ahead of your departure will provide you with increased confidence, and may help you to feel that you are making a positive start towards accomplishing your goal. However, if you are feeling overwhelmed by numerous other aspects of preparing for a major house move and transition, you may not be able to offer your course your full attention, and you might feel disheartened. It will also be important to choose a reputable course as you do not want to develop poor habits that will become difficult to rectifying long term. The alternative is to wait and take a course once you have arrived. This is probably a good idea regardless of whether you have had lessons previously.

Religion

In Britain, we are taught and encouraged to show tolerance and respect for religious beliefs, regardless of how different they are to our own. This is a valuable perspective to maintain while abroad, however, it would be naive to assume that everyone you meet will share this philosophy.

Many countries, such as Australia, Canada, New Zealand and the United States, are familiar with immigration as it has played such a large role in their history. These countries tend to be very tolerant towards each individual having the right to practise and maintain their own beliefs. It is important to do your research about the cultural reactions to your faith before you emigrate. Unfortunately, religion does generate strong reactions from certain groups of people, and it would not be pleasant to instigate such a reaction.

Media and communications

One of the first items on everyone's to-do list when moving house is to ensure their Internet and phone are transferred smoothly. Moving abroad may leave you in cold sweats while imagining trying to negotiate a foreign BT engineer. Whether you run a business from home, or simply want to connect with family abroad on Skype, being online is as necessary as having a refrigerator in most British households. As globalisation has led to many countries expanding their businesses abroad, you may be happy to find local providers in your new location. Vodafone offers both mobile broadband and mobile phone services in 81 different countries.

Thankfully, the Internet is widely available and generally quite good quality.

Australia's most well-known Internet provider is Telstra Bigpond, though like in many industrialised countries there is a wide variety of service providers from which to choose. While there are still many people running their Internet on dial-up connections, broadband is becoming more common. Just like in Britain you will be asked to sign a contract of at least 12 months, and may be charged a fee if you change your mind. Arranging for your connection is simple, all you have to do is call the service provider of your choice. It can be a bit of wait if you need to have the Internet connected in a new property as you will require the assistance of an engineer.

Orcon has the best customer service reputation in New Zealand and offers a range of broadband services from dial-up to satellite or cable, depending on the speed and usage requirements of its customers. Internet packages are often quite limited in comparison to the UK, though satellite and unlimited packages are available if you are willing to pay for it.

Both Canada and the United States are well connected both to the Internet and with quality phone services. Bell, Rogers and TELUS are leading services providers who provide competitive rates.

France and Spain both have relatively few households, which have Internet installed in comparison to Britain. The consequence is that the Internet is still relatively expensive, and broadband is not available in all areas. In Spain, the standard Internet provider is Telefónica, and in France, both Alice and Neuf are recommended.

Internet accessibility extends beyond just being able to get online. In many parts of the world, there are strict bans on what can be accessed. Places such as Saudi Arabia are well known for their strict limits and content bans. In Saudi Arabia, all methods of communication are available almost exclusively through the Saudi Telecom Company.

What many may not expect is that there are many similar, though significantly less strict, regulatory regimes in countries all over the world, including Australia. This will not be a major problem for most people as these bans focus on illegal activities and child pornography. Nonetheless, if you happen to be a researcher on a topic that is controlled, it could mean you need to find an alternate source of information.

Waste and recycling

Most countries are keen to encourage their citizens to recycle. It is very unusual not to have a recycling initiative in place and for there to be rules regarding what should be recycled instead of being disposed. When you arrive in your new home, you will need to contact your local council regarding their specific rubbish and recycling schemes. It is almost universal in major cities and large built-up areas for there to be kerbside rubbish and recycling collections. However, in many countries there are vast areas which are sparsely populated. In these areas, you will be responsible for taking your rubbish to a local tip.

Certain countries do not include waste management as a part of their local council's responsibilities. In these instances, you may need to contact a private waste management company who provides collection services in your area. It is important to ensure you always pay your waste collection company on time as they can be quick to terminate their services. Regardless, of whether the council takes responsibility for your rubbish collections, they will readily fine anyone who allows their rubbish to build up outside their property.

'Most countries are keen to encourage their citizens to recycle.'

Services and utilities

Electricity

Before you pack your belongings, you will have to choose which electrical items you wish to take, and those which will have to be replaced. Most countries use either 120 volts or 230 volts; however, there are a number of countries which use 100, 110, 115, 220 or 240 volts. Laptops tend to be easily modified through the use of an electrical adaptor. Nonetheless, there will be certain items which simply can't be adapted to suit a different electrical system. Never try to use a foreign electrical item without an adaptor – at best, you will trip the power in your building, at worst, you will have an electrical fire. It is also very likely that your electrical appliance will not survive the experience.

Each country may have a specific plug, as well as using a specific voltage.

- Australia runs their electrical system on 230 volts.

- Canada's electrical system uses 110-120 volts.

- France uses 220-240 volts to run their electrical system.

- New Zealand runs their electrical system on 230-240 volts.

- Spain uses 220 volts for their electrical system.

- The United Arab Emirates uses 240 volts for their electrical system.

- The United States runs their electrical system on 120 volts.

Gas

It is very common to have your home heated by gas, whether you are in Britain, Canada or Australia. If gas is commonly used in your area, then it tends to be mains supplied. However, in rural and outlying areas you may have to buy your gas in bottles. Even in the case that you require bottled gas, it is unusual for your gas not to be delivered directly to your door.

Water

It is unusual for clean drinking water not to be available directly to your home in the vast majority of countries. Nonetheless, there are many countries in which expatriates express a strong preference for bottled drinking water. This includes the United Arab Emirates and Spain. In certain countries, such as Spain, it is common to have water shortages in the summer months. In colder climates, it is not unusual to have water shortages due to frozen pipes and waterlines.

'No place is absolutely free from crime.'

Crime and police

Every major city will have its share of problems with crime. Whether it be petty theft and pickpocketing or bank fraud through ATMs. It is important to exercise caution while you become familiar with your new area and the risks that are prevalent. The truth is no place is absolutely free from crime. There will always be someone who behaves inappropriately and spoils it for everyone else.

Be wary of online expatriate scams and be cautious about to whom you release your personal documents. Equally, it is worth taking the advice of your local estate agent should they caution you on choosing a property in an undesirable area. Until you are confident in your ability to appraise the potential problems in your new area, it is in your best interests to choose to live in areas which are deemed safe by local residents.

Before you emigrate, take the time to research the laws in your destination country. Occasionally, expatriates find themselves in trouble for laws with which they were not familiar.

It is inevitable that your destination country will have a slightly different legal system to the one with which you are familiar. The best anyone considering emigration can do is to learn as much as possible about the specific judicial system which they will be relying upon. Try not to worry, as all judicial systems are designed with the ideology of maintaining peace and bringing justice to those who threaten that peace.

Law enforcement is not always respected in every community. Nonetheless, it is always best to show respect to local authorities and to take care to adhere to the laws that are in place. In general, the people who choose to serve their country and communities do so out of a desire to protect the vulnerable and to bring about positive change.

Summing Up

- Before you travel, ensure all your pet's immunisations are up to date and that you have all the correct paperwork.

- There are many countries which will require you to be able to speak the national language before you are allowed to become a citizen.

- Learning a language will broaden the range of opportunities available to you and will allow you assimilate more readily in your new community.

- Most countries are relatively tolerant towards other people's religious beliefs. though, it is always best to approach any religious topic with sensitivity as it generates such intense emotions.

- Internet and phone services should be both reliable and easy to access in your new home. The trend is to have many competing service providers from which customers can choose.

- It is very likely that your electrical goods will require an adaptor in order to function correctly in another country.

- Apply the same rules that you practise when travelling to your first few weeks in your new home. Be wary of petty theft and damaged ATMs. Once you are settled, you will be aware of any potential dangers. The likelihood is that the risk of crime is not any more significant than it is in Britain.

Chapter 9

Healthcare

Before you go

It will be important to request copies of your medical records well in advance of your departure. You will also want to ensure that you have a signed letter from your GP stating any prescriptions you take on a regular basis. Request that your GP provides you with four weeks of your normal medications in advance of your departure. This will allow you to travel and settle without an immediate sense of urgency regarding your health.

Before you leave, you may need vaccinations that are not on the normal British schedule. It is also a good idea to check and ensure you are up to date with all your immunisations. It can seem unnecessary to have extra vaccines, nonetheless, it is in your best interests in order to protect yourself from disease. If you are emigrating to Canada, you will want to have a vaccine for hepatitis B. It is also advisable to familiarise yourself with the most common diseases. Lyme disease is not unusual for those who live rurally due to the generosity of the large tick population. In certain areas, mosquitos are exceptionally dense, and they may carry West Nile fever. For those emigrating to Australia, it is recommended that you have a yellow fever vaccine as well as several others depending upon the area you're moving to and activities in which you wish to participate.

'Ensure that you have a signed letter from your GP stating any prescriptions you take on a regular basis.'

Local healthcare

Australia

Australia is well known for its excellent healthcare system. Using a combination of private and public services, the Australian government develops, regulates and delivers a comprehensive service for all. Every citizen and resident in Australia is covered through the national Medicare programme and the pharmaceutical benefits scheme, regardless of income. Private healthcare is available for those who wish to purchase coverage for it. Unfortunately, those who live on Norfolk Island are not covered by the Medicare programme. Once you have your documentation that proves you have the right to stay in the country, you will need to download an application from the Medicare website, and send it in with all your supporting documents. Many countries do not have the free ambulance service which Britain provides. Australia's ambulance service, physiotherapy and many health aids, such as glasses and hearing aids, are not covered by the Medicare programme. In case of emergency, the emergency assistance number for ambulance, police and fire is 000.

Canada

Canada and the United States share the same emergency services number. Should you require an ambulance, police or fire services, you need to dial 911. The Canadian healthcare system is pretty good. There is a publicly funded system which provides a base level of healthcare for everyone. This Medicare system requires everyone to apply for a healthcare card. Your healthcare card is dependent upon the province in which you reside. If you visit another province, you will be eligible for healthcare, but only as a visitor. The Medicare system is not free, and everyone is expected to pay a nominal monthly fee. When you initially enter Canada, you will not be eligible to apply for a healthcare card until you have lived in the country for an average of 6 months, though this varies slightly from province to province. Prescriptions, ambulance services, physiotherapy and many other services provided by the NHS are not paid for by the Medicare system. Many people pay for private health insurance. It is also very common for employers to provide private medical coverage for their employees and their families. For anyone who requires medical attention outside of normal GP office hours, or should you not currently be registered with a GP, you may attend a walk-in clinic. Walk-in clinics provide wraparound care and will refer to you to any hospital services that you require.

Canada is very protective of those with disabilities. Both the federal and local authorities will offer help with benefits, medical costs, housing and more. In urban areas, there is a programme called HandyDART, which provides a door-to-door specially adapted taxi service, though you must register in advance.

Spain

In order to be eligible for low-cost healthcare, Spanish residents must be registered with the department of social security. Once you have registered, you will be provided with a certificate which will allow you to apply for a Tarjeta Sanitaria Individual (TSI), which is a health card. The TSI covers roughly three-quarters of the cost of medical treatments and prescriptions. The remaining portion of costs must be met individually or through private medical insurance. If you need emergency medical, fire or police services, the number you need to call is 112. Anyone who holds a Spanish social security card or a European Health Insurance Card will be entitled to free emergency treatment in a state hospital. In Spanish hospitals, it is assumed that family or private carers will provide any care needed. Medical staff will provide only medical treatments. Generally, you will not need any further immunisations, provided your British vaccine history is complete. Hepatitis B is recommended for anyone who may come into contact with wild animals such as bats, though it is not mandatory. Most pharmacies in Spain are open from 9:30 to 21:30, with a three-hour break between two and five o'clock. The pharmacy sign is a green cross, which is identical to the pharmacy signs posted in the UK. Spanish pharmacies provide many medications over the counter with simply the advice of a pharmacist, instead of requiring a prescription, such as antibiotics. Should you visit the hospital and require medicine at home, you will receive a medical report which you must take to your GP. Your GP will then issue you with a prescription to take to a pharmacy. Dentists in Spain are exclusively private, though the charges are comparatively reasonable, and the quality of the treatment is reported to be excellent.

New Zealand

New Zealand's healthcare is very well reputed. The standard of care and reputation for maintaining a strong network of outstanding medical professionals is repeatedly confirmed by those who live there. Healthcare is not free at the point of service like it is with the NHS. When you visit your GP, you will be charged a fee. Each GP is allowed to set their own fees, though these are subsidised by the government. The Primary Health Organisation works with registered doctors to provide affordable care. It is common for patients to shop around before selecting a GP. Children who are under the age of six are exempt from paying for treatment within normal practice hours. Women who are pregnant receive free healthcare for the duration of their pregnancy, birth and aftercare. Anyone in receipt of benefits or on a low income is eligible for a Community Services Card to reduce the cost of treatment. All emergency treatment is funded by the Accident Compensation Corporation. Hence, there is no need to worry should you be in an accident that you will not receive excellent care. Should you be in need of the emergency services the number to call is 111. Equally, all essential hospital care is free of charge. Many people in New Zealand opt for private healthcare and there are a wide range of medical insurance policies available. If you are in need of seeing your GP more than 12 times a year, you can apply for a High Use Health Card which allows you to see your GP at a discount.

'New Zealand's healthcare is very well reputed.'

Non-residents will be charged for all treatments, although accidents are generally free for anyone, regardless of their residency status. There is no formal registration for New Zealand health services and subsequently you do not need to apply for a healthcare card.

Medications are relatively tightly regulated in New Zealand. Certain medications which are approved for use in the UK, are not yet available. Other medications which are available over the counter in Britain, are only available on prescription. Prescriptions are charged at a standard rate of $15, however, specialist prescriptions are often more expensive. Residents who qualify for a discount will only be charged $3 per prescription.

All your UK vaccines need to be up to date before departure, and it is recommended that everyone be vaccinated for hepatitis B. Anyone who is planning on going to the Pacific Islands should consider being immunised for hepatitis A and typhoid. Insects bites can carry Ross River virus and Murray Valley encephalitis. Both of which are worth being aware of and taking proper precautions to prevent.

France

Healthcare in France is very good. The quality of care between state run and private hospitals is nearly identical. France's healthcare leads the way with the ideology that patients come first and that all residents have access to adequate medical care. For all treatment, you will be required to present a carte vitale (a health insurance card), and you will typically have to pay a fee. The public health insurance programme covers all legal residents of France, and from which you will be refunded between 70-95% of your treatment costs. The French government ensures that those who need refunds receive them promptly. There are many conditions that are entitled to a 100% refund; these are not limited to but include pregnancy and childbirth, cancer and diabetes. For those on low income, financial aid is available through the revenu minimum d'insertion. EU citizens must be making a contribution to the social security system in order to access all areas of the healthcare system. Should you require emergency services in France, the number to call is 112.

In order to ease the burden on the healthcare system, everyone in France is urged to try non-prescription medications before going directly to prescriptions. This is due to most prescriptions being eligible for up to a 100% refund. The first time you visit a pharmacy they will ask you to register, and show them your carte vitale.

Dubai

While the facilities available in Dubai are considered to be excellent, it is advised that you invest in private medical insurance. Doctors offer patient-centered care to everyone, regardless of nationality or residency. However, you will be expected to pay for your treatment upfront and to seek reimbursement from your insurance company.

United States

It is well known that the United States do not have a free comprehensive medical programme, however, in an emergency you will always be treated first, and asked to pay before you leave. It is relatively normal to have to pay a certain percentage of your fee upfront and to be reimbursed by your insurance afterwards. Please do not assume that it is affordable to pay as you need treatment to avoid insurance premiums. It is not unusual for an ambulance to cost $300 per mile. If you are in a rural area, you may be 40 miles from the hospital. While you will not be charged upfront, an uninsured ambulance bill through your door a month afterwards could cause a heart attack! Emergency services are available by calling 911, however, most people will understandably avoid calling an ambulance unless it is really unavoidable. If you are going into the hospital as an emergency but are able to get there without an ambulance, you will want to call to let them know you are coming. It is frequently possible to be given an appointment or at least placed in the queue which will avoid you having to wait hours to be treated. It is very common for most Americans to be insured through a medical insurance plan provided by their employer. While there are healthcare programmes such as Medicare, it is unlikely that you will be eligible. Due to the nature of medical care in America, doctors tend to treat their patients more like customers. If you feel you need a certain type of prescription or a certain kind of treatment, an American doctor's far more likely to take your request seriously as you are paying for your treatment.

Prescription medications must be paid for and are all too often tearfully expensive for anyone who is not insured. Ensure that the medical insurance you take out will cover at least some of your prescription costs.

Insurance policies

You will need to do your research before choosing an insurance policy. There are many kinds of coverage and policies that may be provided from a private company or from a governing body. Many policies do not cover medications or alternative treatments. Certain prescription medications will cost more than the visit to the doctor. Only you will be able to decide the level of coverage with which you feel comfortable.

Working abroad

In many countries, it is common for employers to provide you with medical coverage for the duration of your employment. This coverage should also extend to cover your dependents. However, many of these policies are not inclusive, and you may require further insurance to meet your needs.

Pharmacies and medicine

Unfortunately, the names of medications are not universal. It will take a while to become familiar with new names of the medication you require. Paracetamol is known as acetaminophen in the United States and Canada, apiretal in Spain, and doliprane in France. Diazepam is sold as antenex in Australia. Many of these are sold under specific brand names, which can make finding what you are looking for difficult. If you are taking any medication on a regular basis, it is worth doing a quick Internet search to find the name and availability of your medication in your destination country. This will allow you to enter your new situation prepared and able to take charge of your healthcare.

Don't hesitate to ask a pharmacist for help. They are very knowledgable, and in many countries they are qualified to offer you advice similar to a doctor. It is very important that you read all the information provided with any medication you are buying for the first time. While you are probably familiar with how to take ibuprofen in the UK, in Dubai, ibuprofen is frequently sold in 800mg tablets. These are four times the dose of their British equivalent and should not be taken two at a time.

Each country will vary regarding their medicinal availability. In some countries, you can buy large quantities of drugs over the counter that are controlled in Britain. In others, you will find that medications you did not require a prescription for in the UK are regulated as prescription only.

While it is always worth checking before you travel, it is generally accepted that you may take a four-week supply of any medications you are currently taking with you. It will be important to have your doctor write a letter on your behalf regarding all medications you are prescribed on a regular basis.

'In many countries, it is common for employers to provide you with medical coverage for the duration of your employment.'

Summing Up

- You will need to request a copy of your medical records and ensure you have any necessary vaccines ahead of departure.

- Research and apply for private healthcare before you emigrate. In most cases, you will want to have private healthcare as there are very few places that have free comprehensive medical coverage.

- Your employer may provide you with health insurance as a part of your employment contract. However, this may not provide inclusive coverage.

- Read any insurance policy carefully to ensure it provides coverage that meets your needs.

- Medication names are not universal. In addition, medication doses are not universal, and as such you should always read the instructions before taking medication dispensed in a foreign country.

Chapter 10

Transport

Getting there

Once you have a rough date of departure, you will be able to book your flights. Unless you prefer long-distance rail or coach travel and are heading to a European destination, you are likely to be taking an airline to your chosen destination. Every country tends to be served by a national, and often more expensive, airline, as well as cheaper budget airlines. While budget airlines may at first appear cheaper that choosing a national airline, such as Quantas if you are going to Australia, it tends to be worth your while to take a national flight. There will be less hassle with add-on fees, a more lenient luggage allowance, and the flight times tend to be far more reasonable.

'An often overlooked route is to travel on a freight ship.'

There is the possibility of travelling by sea if you prefer. You may have already travelled to France by ferry, but should you be going further afield there are still a number of options available. There are cruises liners, which can take you from the UK all the way to Australia. It is possible to take a cruise liner to Canada or the UAE, however, it uncommon for the cruise route to commence from a UK port.

An often overlooked route is to travel on a freight ship. There are many routes that stop at a port in the UK or in Europe and are willing to carry passengers. Freight ships are not designed as luxury holiday boats and as such tend to have cabins available for only a dozen extra passengers. The accommodation is comparable to Travelodge and rooms will have fridges, televisions and en-suite bathrooms. There will not be the wide range of on-board activities that you would expect to find on board a commercial cruise liner, but there tends to be a small selection of activities in which to participate. The costs associated with freight ships tend to be in the region of £100 per day and include meals and accommodation.

If you want to build a vacation into your move, it is certainly possible, and will be well earned once all your packing is complete.

Documentation

Before you will be allowed to enter any new country, you will have to hold either a visa or a passport to the destination country. If you are taking any children, you will be asked to show confirmation of parental responsibility. Any items that you are shipping to your destination will need to be listed in detail, along with their monetary value. Ideally, you should take any receipts you have for every item in order to show that it has been in your possession for at least 12 months.

You will also want to have copies of proof of your financial situation. It is not unusual to be stopped at the border and asked to prove your ability to support yourself, despite having already been approved for a visa.

It is common for individuals to be asked to prove that they are in good health and that they have received certain immunisations. As well as a copy of your medical records it is worth taking a copy of your immunisation record and a letter from your doctor regarding any conditions you may have.

If you are travelling with pets, you will need to have all their documentation with you as well. Everything from their health records to their passports will be checked before you are cleared for entry.

It is important to keep any letters of confirmation regarding employment, housing or education to prove your reasons for entering the country.

This can seem very tiresome and a little overwhelming. There is every chance that you may not be asked to see anything further than your passport, however, in the case that you are stopped and requested to show further information, you will be relieved to be able to produce the information they are requesting. It is unlikely that you will be asked every time you come and go, nonetheless, it is always better to keep all the evidence which may be requested to hand. In today's fearful state, where borders are constantly on alert for terrorism and illegal immigrants, government officials are driven to be exceptionally careful of whom they allow entry.

Removals and storage

There are lots of international moving companies available. It is very worthwhile to shop around as their quotes will vary enormously. Don't hesitate to contact smaller local firms in either the UK or your destination country. It is not always the case that a larger firm will provide the better service for a lower fee.

Anything you choose to ship will be subject to customs inspection and potential duties. Most countries do not charge duty on personal items that have been owned and in use for at least 12 months. It is possible for you to be asked to show proof of purchase on items you are taking. Collect as many receipts as possible and keep them with your documents for safe keeping. Anything you ship must be clean, for example, if you are shipping gardening tools that are still covered in soil, they will in all likelihood be rejected. Each country will have its own list of forbidden items, but they tend to be very similar, listing items such as soil, animal skins, weapons and drugs.

Cars and motoring

It is always a good idea to apply for your international driving licence ahead of leaving Britain. Most countries will allow you to continue to drive on your British licence for a while. New Zealand will not expect you to change your licence for 12 months, however, Australia will expect you to apply for an Australian licence after three months. Nonetheless, an international driving licence does have benefits from being an accepted form of identification to being better received by officials should you need to show proof of your licence. Most English-speaking countries will allow you to transfer your licence directly over to their national licence without taking another test. However, if you do not have a licence, you will have to comply with their licence application process.

Contacting your new DVLA office and requesting a copy of their rules and signs will make driving an easier transition. There will be differences that take time to develop your confidence before you will feel at ease driving again. In many countries, you will need to practise driving on the opposite side of the road. Speed limits, stop signs, and common driving cues may all vary from those that are familiar to you. Equally, it can be quite a challenge having to navigate and learn your way around a new area while practising new road skills. Many people do opt for taking a couple of driving courses to allow them

'It is always a good idea to apply for your international driving licence ahead of leaving Britain.'

the chance to practise. While it may feel redundant, taking lessons will also allow you to encounter and better understand the public mindset towards driving and the role you take on as a fellow driver. Some places see drivers as having a duty of care towards all pedestrians, and expect everyone to acknowledge and drive with a view towards their interests. Others drivers drive very aggressively, and if you perform less assertively you may generate a lot of hostility.

The next major hurdle to overcome is parking. Parking rules vary almost as much as local cuisine varies between continents. In France, there are roads where you may park on one side of the street on certain days, and on others you may only park on the opposite side. In Australia, you may not park on a nature strip, and there are many areas where the parking is for residents only.

Most countries have car parks and metered parking spots. Until you are familiar with the local parking nuances, it is best to avoid trying to park freely. Most places will simply issue you with a parking fine, however, in many places you may come back to find your vehicle has been towed and impounded, without so much as a letter or phone number remaining to tell you where and what you should do next.

Public transport

Many larger countries, such as Canada, the United States and France, do not have very much in the way of national bus services. The distances are so large that trains tend to make up the bulk of the travelling. In many of the largest cities, there are excellent bus services, however, there are so many large open areas with little population that it is not affordable or practical to maintain regular routes. In such areas, the only method of transport is by car. If you are living in a major city, then you will have excellent access to one or more methods of public transit. In Vancouver, Canada, you will have the option of riding the sky train, the sea bus, or taking one of an excellent network of buses. However, just an hour outside the city, there are many rural towns which have no public transport whatsoever.

Summing Up

- National airlines tend to have generous luggage allowances and reasonable flight times. When you are already dealing with the stress of moving house, it may be worth paying a little bit extra.

- You must have the following documents available for inspection before you will be permitted to enter your destination country: passport and visa, proof of finances, medical records, pet documents and proof of parental responsibility.

- Shop around to ensure you find an affordable removal company, and ask if they will supply the appropriate customs documents.

- An international driving licence will allow you to drive for 12 months in another country and provides an accepted form of identification.

- The availability of public transportation is dependent upon population density and resources. Most major cities have good transportation systems in place, however if you are in a rural area, it is likely that you will need a car.

Glossary

Affidavit

Is a signed oath that is witnessed by a solicitor or notary.

Affidavit of Support

This refers to the paperwork you are required to show to prove you have adequate means to support yourself and any family members.

Affirmation of allegiance

This is an official declaration or oath where an applicant for citizenship pledges their allegiance to their new country, government or monarch.

Asylum

Asylum is granted to an asylee. An asylee is granted protection due to a fear of persecution should they return to their homeland.

Border

This is the place where two countries meet.

Commonwealth

This is a voluntary association of 53 independent countries that work together to promote international understanding, in the common interests of their people.

Conditional permanent resident

Anyone granted conditional permanent residence will be allowed the same rights and responsibilities as a permanent resident. However, they must apply to have their conditions removed in order to gain permanent residence status.

Descent

Citizenship gained through your parents or in certain circumstance grandparents.

Emigrate

When a person has permanently left their home country to live in a different country.

Expatriate (Expat)

The name given to someone who lives in a country which is not their birthplace.

Entry clearance

In order to be given permission to travel or enter you will require entry clearance documents.

Immigrate

When a person has come to a new country to permanently reside.

Immigration status

This is the legal position which clarifies whether your right to remain in a country has restrictions.

Integration

This is the process of building a life for yourself and acting as an established member of a community.

Need2Know

Nationality

This can be the same as your citizenship, however it is possible to hold a nationality, without being a citizen. For example, British nationals but not British citizens.

Naturalisation

This is the legal process by which you become a citizen of a country and are granted the same rights as someone who was born in the country.

Notary

This is a public official who has the legal authorisation to witness the signing of documents and perform formal duties.

Refugee

A person who has a fear that they will be subject to persecution due to their race, religion, nationality, or social or political opinion.

Right of abode

This is the legal right to live and work in a given country.

Sponsor

A sponsor is someone who assumes responsibility within certain limitations during a specific period of time.

Appendix

Complete Moving Checklist

Six months in advance

Contact the consulate of your destination country to enquire about:	Done
Vaccine requirements	
Visas	
Work permits	
Registration requirements	
Necessary documentation	
Customs duties	
Items which are prohibited	
Pet requirements	
Taxes	
Available housing options	
Educational institutions	
Publications that target new residents	
Local council information	

Two months in advance

Ensure the following documents are ready for travel and renew any which will soon expire.	Done
Passport	
Birth certificate	
Book travel tickets	
Adoption papers	
Marriage certificate	
International driver's licence	
Educational records	
Banking records	
Property deeds	
Wills and inheritance paperwork	
Jewellery valuations	
Insurance papers	
Pet's health records	

Six weeks in advance

To do:	Done
Ship items that you are sending ahead.	
Arrange banking in your new country.	
Have notarised copies made of all your important documents	
Arrange your post to be forwarded to your new address.	
Sort through your belongings and begin selling what you do not need.	
Visit your GP for any vaccines which you require.	
Purchase health insurance.	
Finalise any travel plans and ensure rental cars and plane tickets are booked.	
Make contact with child(ren)'s school, if necessary.	
Make all arrangements on behalf of your pets.	

Four weeks in advance

Contact the following service providers to notify them of the discontinuation of your services.	Done
Gas	
Electricity	
Water	
Telephone	
Internet	
Council tax	
Mobile phone	
Newspapers and magazines	
Local insurance companies	
Store cards	
TV licence	

Two weeks in advance

To do:	Done
Visit your GP for a prescription for 4 weeks' worth of any medications which you take regularly.	
Start using up the contents of your freezer and cupboard.	
Make any final arrangements for your moving day.	
Begin cleaning both the garden and interior of the house.	
Organise your clothing and take items you no longer need to the charity shop.	
Perform a final check to ensure all your documents are in order and safely stored together.	

Day before

To do:	Done
Charge your mobile phone.	
Defrost your freezer and fridge.	
Pack your luggage.	
Label your keys.	
Separate out any items which are to remain at the property.	
Take away all excess rubbish.	
Tidy and clean the property.	

On the day

To do:	Done
Ensure all documents are safely stored away.	
Take meter readings.	
Switch off the power and water.	
Clear the house and leave the keys with the estate agent.	
Take care of yourself by eating and drinking regularly.	

Help List

Online forums/websites

ASA Group

http://www.australia-migration.com/
ASA is a business which provides migration services to those who would like
to emigrate to Australia. Their website contains some valuable information,
regardless of whether or not you choose to use their services.

Bye Bye Blighty

http://www.byebyeblighty.com
This website has information on emigrating to Australia, Canada, New Zealand,
Spain and the United States from Britain.

CanadaVisa.com

http://www.canadavisa.com
Campbell Cohen Law Firm, 1980 Sherbrooke Street West, Suite 800, Montreal,
QC, Canada, H3H 1E8
Tel: + 1 514 937 9445
This site features a wealth of articles and essays on immigrating to Canada.

Emigrate.co.uk

http://www.emigrate.co.uk/
A website featuring over 300 helpful articles on emigrating from the United
Kingdom. From the website, you can access their blog and forums.

Emigrate New Zealand

http://www.emigratenz.co.uk/
A site dedicated to supplying information specifically aimed at British
emigrants.

Emigration Expert

http://www.emigrationexpert.co.uk/
While this site is not as comprehensive as some of the others, it does provide a good introduction to a wide range of topics that pertain to emigration.

EmigratingtoAustralia.com

http://www.emigratingtoaustralia.com/
For Australia specific information on many topics, including case studies, it is worth looking at this site.

Emigrate2

http://www.emigrate2.co.uk/
Emigrate2 is an information hub for all aspects of living and working abroad.

Expat Focus

http://www.expatfocus.com/
Providing plenty of information, this website covers everything from financial advice to first-hand experiences. There is also a forum available through the website.

Go work abroad

http://www.goworkabroad.co.uk/
Green Wood Drive, Manor Park, Cheshire, WA7 1UP
This website contains information on finding employment and working abroad.

INTSTUDY.com

http://www.intstudy.com/
127-129 Great Suffolk Street, London, SE1 1PP
This is an excellent online resource which addresses every aspect of studying abroad.

New Zealand's Information Network

http://www.nz-immigration.co.nz/
PO Box 327, Rangiora 7440, New Zealand

While this company is dedicated to promoting New Zealand for tourism purposes, this website is a great resource for anyone considering moving to New Zealand.

Prism XPAT

http://www.prismxpat.co.uk/
Hamilton House, Mabledon Place, London, WC1H 9BB
Tel: 0845 450 4004
This company website offers advice and financial planning information for anyone considering a move abroad.

Property-abroad.com

http://www.property-abroad.com/
9 College Close, Dalton Piercy, Hartlepool, Cleveland, TS27 3JA
Tel: 0845 2000 467
Founded by Les Calvert, this site was created with the intention of bringing resources regarding the purchase and sale of properties internationally together. There are helpful guides divided by country and a property search engine.

Safe Travel

http://www.safetravel.co.uk
This site offers an abundance of information and advice on travel and immigration. All the information is divided up into a specific section based on location and topic.

Transitions Abroad.com

http://www.transitionsabroad.com/
This website contains lots of helpful articles on everything from volunteering abroad to travelling with pets.

Professional Organisations

Citizenship and Immigration Canada

http://www.cic.gc.ca/
Tel: 1 888 242 2100
This site features information given by the government of Canada on all aspects of immigrating and naturalising.

New Zealand Visa Bureau

http://www.visabureau.com/
15 Harwood Road, London, England, SW6 4QP
This is an independent UK-based immigration advisory service that specialises in visa and immigration to New Zealand.

UAE Immigration Departments

http://www.dubaifaqs.com/immigration-uae.php
This is not a pretty website, but it has a useful list of official contacts within the UAE immigration department.

U.S. Department of State-A Service of The Bureau of Consular Affairs

http://travel.state.gov
This site provides detailed information for immigrants to the United States. There are detailed explanations for individual visa categories and information on laws and regulations.

Book List

Freedom to move and live in Europe

European Commission (Available at: http://ec.europa.eu/justice/policies/citizenship/docs/guide_free_movement_low.pdf)

Immigration

Global Issues (Available at: http://www.globalissues.org/article/537/immigration)

How To Buy Overseas Property Safely 2013

The Consumer Guide From the Industry Body (Available at: http://content.yudu.com/Library/A1zc0h/AIPP2013directory/resources/index.htm?referrerUrl=http://free.yudu.com/item/details/630574/AIPP-2013-directory)

Immigration and social cohesion in the UK

Joseph Rowntree Foundation (Available at: http://www.jrf.org.uk/sites/files/jrf/2230-deprivation-cohesion-immigration.pdf)

References

Citizenship and Immigration Canada [Online] Available at:
http://www.cic.gc.ca/english/citizenship/become.asp [accessed on 10 May 2013]

Department of Health [Online] Available at:
http://www.dh.gov.uk [accessed on 7 May 2013]

ExpatFocus [Online] Available at: http://www.expatfocus.com/
[accessed on 30 April 2013]

ExpatForum [Online]
Available at: http://www.expatforum.com/articles/health/health-care-in-dubai.html
[accessed on 12 May 2013]

Home Office UK Boarder Agency [Online]
Available at: http://www.ukba.homeoffice.gov.uk/glossary?letter=U
[accessed on 6 May 2013]

Petsandtravel [Online] Available at: http://www.petsandtravel.co.uk/
[accessed on 6 May 2013]

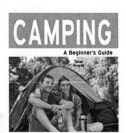

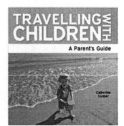